Alexander Charles Ewald

The Crown and its Advisers or Queen, Ministers, Lords, & Commons

Alexander Charles Ewald

The Crown and its Advisers or Queen, Ministers, Lords, & Commons

ISBN/EAN: 9783337267254

Printed in Europe, USA, Canada, Australia, Japan

Cover: Foto ©ninafisch / pixelio.de

More available books at **www.hansebooks.com**

THE CROWN

AND

ITS ADVISERS

THE CROWN

AND

ITS ADVISERS

OR

QUEEN, MINISTERS, LORDS, & COMMONS

BY

ALEX. CHARLES EWALD, F.S.A.

(OF HER MAJESTY'S RECORD OFFICE)

AUTHOR OF THE 'GUIDE TO THE CIVIL SERVICE,' 'LAST CENTURY
OF UNIVERSAL HISTORY,' ETC.

WILLIAM BLACKWOOD AND SONS
EDINBURGH AND LONDON
MDCCCLXX

TO

His Grace the Duke of Richmond, K.G.

PRESIDENT OF THE "NATIONAL UNION OF CONSERVATIVE
ASSOCIATIONS,"

&c. &c. &c.

THESE LECTURES

ARE BY SPECIAL PERMISSION DEDICATED

BY HIS FAITHFUL SERVANT

THE AUTHOR.

PREFACE.

THESE Lectures were delivered by me last winter, at the request of the "National Union of Conservative Associations," to various audiences of Conservative working-men, both in London and the country. As my only object in writing them was to extend to my fellow-countrymen a knowledge of the leading *facts* and principles of our Constitution, I endeavoured, as far as possible, to avoid giving expression to anything like party-feeling, and confined my attempts to placing before my hearers those salient points in our system of Government, without some knowledge of which no man can be considered justly entitled to give an opinion on political questions.

The temperate tone I studied to maintain throughout these Lectures was approved by audiences that included, besides Conservatives, Liberals of all shades of opinions.

It is hoped that the 'Crown and its Advisers' may serve as a useful constitutional Manual, and be the means of causing many to examine more fully for themselves the working of that great machine, the State. If it should help to make our working-classes understand a whit better the nature of the constitution under which they have the happiness to live, and induce them to search for themselves the pages of our great constitutional authorities, instead of being content with mere "clap-trap" opinions, the object of the Author will be most fully gained.

It only remains for me to make my grateful acknowledgments to the writers on our Constitution and its History from whose rich stores I have so freely drawn, and to whose antecedent labours these Lectures are indebted for their existence. The following is a list of

the chief authorities I have consulted: May's
'*Constitutional History*' and '*Parliamentary
Practice;*' Cox's '*Institutions of the English
Government;*' Alpheus Todd, '*On Parliamentary Government in England;*' Hallam's
'*Constitutional History of England;*' Blackstone's '*Commentaries on the Laws of England;*' the Histories of England by Hume,
Lingard, and Mackintosh; Cooke's 'History
of Party;' Earl Grey, 'On Parliamentary
Government;' R. Palgrave's 'Lectures on the
House of Commons;' R. Dudley Baxter's
'English Parties and Conservatism;' De
Lolme, 'On the Constitution,' edited by
Stephens; Dod's 'Parliamentary Companion;' 'Encyclopædia Britannica;' and various constitutional articles in the Edinburgh,
Quarterly, and Saturday Reviews. To those
works in italics I am under the deepest obligations.

JUNIOR CARLTON CLUB,
Oct. 1870.

CONTENTS.

LECTURE	PAGE
I. THE QUEEN,	1
II. THE MINISTRY,	50
III. THE HOUSE OF LORDS,	125
IV. THE COMMONS,	171

THE CROWN

AND

ITS ADVISERS.

LECTURE I.

THE QUEEN.

"The country has a deep-rooted affection for kingly government, and would highly resent any attempt to change or destroy this key-stone of the Constitution: nor, as far as I can observe, is this sentiment confined to particular orders of men; it pervades the whole country, from one end to the other."—EARL RUSSELL, *English Government and Constitution.*

> " A land of just and old renown,
> Where freedom broadens slowly down
> From precedent to precedent."
> —TENNYSON.

GENTLEMEN,—I intend to lecture to you to-night upon the office and prerogatives of her Majesty the Queen. I shall endeavour to show you what power the Crown has in the control of public affairs, and what limits there are to its authority since the introduction of parliamentary government. And here let me tell you at once that such a subject must necessarily be a dry one. Had I to talk to you about the non-political position of our gracious Sovereign, and to give you a biographical sketch of her Majesty, illustrated by different anecdotes of her kindness and benevolence, or to contrast her conduct with that of many of the other Sovereigns who have preceded her, my task would be perhaps a more interesting one. But I come among you to-night, not as an artist who wishes to portray a pleasing picture of royalty, but as an anatomist who has to dissect its rights and privileges, and lay bare all that concerns its political system.

Now I have no doubt you all fancy that you know a good deal about the duties of a Sovereign of England. You hear of her Majesty moving about from one palace to another—now at London, then at Windsor; now at Osborne, and then again at Balmoral. You have seen her driving down to Westminster in royal state to open Parliament, with soldiers escorting her, officers in splendid uniforms waiting on her, and a loyal crowd cheering

"God save the Queen!" And then you read of her giving state balls and dinners, holding drawing-rooms and levees, or else being present at the inauguration of some great event, the observed of all observers, with everything that can flatter human vanity and gratify human ambition surrounding her, and you think what a brilliant and splendid life the Queen's must be. And so it is; but you look upon the brilliant side of it only. You seem to forget that her Majesty has many very important duties to perform, and that the royal life is not one eternal freedom from care, anxiety, and hard work. You forget this; and so, when you wish to typify happiness—and by happiness you mean idleness—you say, as "happy as a queen." Well, my friends, I hope I shall be able to disabuse your minds of this notion, and to show you that to be a king or queen of these realms is not entirely a life of brilliant idleness. And if there are any among you who are accustomed to view with disrespect the position of her Majesty, and to hold derogatory ideas regarding her power and influence—looking upon her as a mere state puppet, and as only a tool in the hands of her ministers — I ask them to listen to me patiently for a little while, and then to see whether they can consistently support such views, and promulgate them as constitutional facts.

But before I can tell you anything of the Queen, I must let you know something about the position she occupies in relation to the British Constitution. Now what is the British Constitution? You hear its name thundered forth on the hustings, at meetings, at debates, and perhaps you talk about it yourselves without understanding very well its meaning. What, then, is this British Constitution? I will try to explain it to you. The political writers of antiquity recognised only three regular forms of government—namely, a *Democracy* in which the sovereign power is vested in the people, as is the case in the United States; *Aristocracy*, in which the supreme power is confined to a few members of the community distinguished by birth or wealth, as was formerly the case in Venice; and *Monarchy*, in which sovereign authority is wielded by a single person, as is the case in Russia, Turkey, &c. These three species of government have all of them their various good and bad points. Democracies are usually best calculated to direct the end of a law, aristocracies to invent the means by which that law is to be obtained, and monarchies to carry those means into execution. The British Constitution, however, conforms to none of the above definitions, but is a *mixed* government formed out of them all, and partaking of the advantages of each. This mixed government we call a *limited monarchy* —that is, a monarchy in which the Crown is not absolute, but must rule according to the usages of the Constitution, and in subjection to the laws of the realm. This form of government is one peculiarly suited to the character and temperament of the British people. A democracy, however popular among certain classes of our nation at first, would soon lose its authority, from the want of that social influence which is so dear to the English in general. No government in England would long continue popular whose members were taken entirely from the sons of the people. On the other hand, a government purely aristocratic would be one little calculated to further the interests of the nation at large, from the nature of its exclusive policy; whilst an absolute monarchy, as the history of England plainly shows, has ever been detested by the people as contrary to the very spirit of our Constitution, for Englishmen are subjects and not slaves. But a government like ours, in which the executive power is lodged in the Sovereign, while the legislative power is intrusted to the Three Estates of the realm,* unites in itself the chief elements of democracy, aristocracy, and absolute monarchy, and hence is the most perfect plan of government that could possibly be adopted, for in no other form could we find a more impartial system of administration. Were the supreme power placed in any one of the three branches separately, we should be exposed to the faults of either absolute monarchy, aristocracy, or democracy. On the other hand, were the supreme power intrusted to any two of these three branches to the exclusion of the third, we should be none the less liable to evils, though of a different kind. If, for instance, all power were confined to the Sovereign and the House of Lords, our laws might be providently made and well executed, but they would not, in all probability, have always the good of the people in view. Again, were the supreme power vested in the Sovereign and the House of Commons, we should want that "circumspection and mediatory caution" which the wisdom of the Peers secures, and which have in many critical cases been exerted to protect the powers

---

* The Three Estates of the realm are the Lords Temporal, the Lords Spiritual, and the Commons—*not* Queen, Lords, and Commons.

of the executive and legislative government from mutual encroachment. And if the supreme rights of legislature were lodged in the two Houses of Parliament only, they might be tempted to abolish the kingly office altogether, or to greatly weaken the executive power. Thus you see how perfectly our constitutional government is united, so that nothing can endanger its welfare save the destruction of those balances of power which maintain the different parts of our complex political system in equipoise. Hence you will, I have no doubt, readily perceive that when we talk about the British Constitution we mean a form of government in which the supreme power is virtually in the laws, though the majesty of government and the administration are vested in a single person. And now, having made these remarks, let us examine the power and office of the Queen.

Succession to the throne of England is hereditary, but with certain limitations, for the right of inheritance may from time to time be changed by Act of Parliament—a power which, you well know, Parliament has exercised in various reigns. Then, again, the title to the throne, since the passing of the Act of Settlement in 1701, is conditional upon the heir-apparent being a member of the Church of England,

and of the issue of the Princess Sophia of Hanover, who was a granddaughter of James I. No one professing the Popish religion, or being married to a Papist, can, by the Bill of Rights, rule over these realms; so that when you hear people talking about the government of Great Britain and Ireland being an hereditary monarchy, you will remember that it is not absolutely hereditary, because it may be subject to limitations by Parliament if necessary, and is conditional upon the heir to the throne being a Protestant, and of a certain family.

I suppose you all are well aware that there is a great Council assembled at Rome to decide whether the Pope is infallible or not; and all of you being stanch Protestants, of course look upon infallibility in man as utter nonsense. But what will you think of me when I tell you that her Majesty is *infallible?*

Yes, that the King or Queen of England can *do no wrong* is one of the great principles of the British Constitution. But this statement need not shock your religious principles, as her Majesty's infallibility is only political; for whatever is exceptionable in the conduct of public affairs is not to be imputed to her, nor is she answerable for it personally to her people. The maxim that the Queen "can do no wrong," though it sounds like a moral paradox, simply means, that if any mismanagement of Government arises, the Queen is not to be blamed, because all acts of the Crown are presumed to have been done by some minister responsible to Parliament. Supposing—indeed it is a supposition!—that her Majesty were to command some unlawful act to be performed, that command would be no excuse to the minister for a wrong administration of power. Lord Danby was impeached by Parliament for a letter which contained a postscript in the King's own handwriting, declaring that that very letter had been written by his command. In order that the Queen may do no wrong, there is not a moment in her life, from her accession to her demise, during which there is not some one responsible to Parliament for her public conduct. The personal actions of her Majesty, not being acts of Government, are not under the cognisance of the law.

But here you must remember that though the Queen is not personally responsible to any human tribunal for the exercise of the functions of royalty, yet these functions are regulated by law, and must be discharged for the public welfare, and not merely to gratify her personal inclinations. In fact, it is an express part of the common law of England that the Sovereign of these realms *must* govern according to law. In the reign of William III. it was declared by statute that the laws of England are the birthright of the English people, and that all kings and queens of this realm, together with their officers and ministers, are to administer the government of the same according to the said laws. And this statute has never been repealed. But long before William III. it had been one of our constitutional maxims that the King of England was never an absolute monarch. Bracton, who flourished in the reign of Henry III., wrote, "It is the law which makes the King. Let the King therefore render to the law what the law has vested in him with regard to others—dominion and power: for he is not truly King where will and pleasure rule, and not the law." And again, "The King also hath a superior—namely, God; and also the law, by which he was made a king." For though the Queen is our sovereign lord, she does not possess the sovereign authority of the commonwealth, because that is vested, not in her Majesty singly, but in the Queen, Lords, and Commons jointly. When her Majesty was crowned Queen of England, she took the following oath, which is called the Coronation Oath:—"*The Archbishop:* 'Will you solemnly promise and swear to govern the people of this kingdom of England, and the dominions thereto belonging, according to the statutes in Parliament agreed on, and the laws and customs of the same?' *The Queen:* 'I solemnly promise so to do.' *Archbishop:* 'Will you to the utmost of your power cause law and justice, in mercy, to be executed in all your judgments?' *Queen:* 'I will.' *Archbishop:* 'Will you to the utmost of your power maintain the laws of God, the true profession of the Gospel, and the Protestant reformed religion established by the law? And will you preserve unto the bishops and clergy of this realm, and to the churches committed to their charge, all such rights and privileges as by law do or shall appertain unto them, or any of them?' *Queen:* 'All this I promise to do.' *After this, the Queen, laying her hand upon the Holy Gospels, said:* 'The things which I have here before promised I will perform and keep: So help me God:' *and then her Majesty kissed the book."*

But an English Sovereign is not only infallible but *immortal.* Now, perhaps, you will think that this is downright nonsense, because you know that our Sovereigns are just as likely to die as the poorest peasant in the land. And if they do not die, what have become of our Norman, Plantagenet, Lancastrian, Yorkist, Tudor, Stuart, and Hanoverian kings? No, say you, we cannot quite swallow that, though we do belong to the "stupid party." But you see, when I told you that the Queen was infallible, I meant only politically; and so when I say that an English Sovereign is immortal, I mean only in a political and not in a natural sense. You have often read of the phrase, the *King never dies;* and it means simply this, that immediately upon the decease of the reigning prince in his natural capacity, his kingly office is vested at once in his heir, who is from that very moment King to all intents and purposes. So you see that it is not the king personally who never dies, but his title and office. When we talk of the demise of the crown, we only mean that in consequence of the disunion of the King's natural body from his body politic, the kingdom is demised or transferred to his successor, and hence the royal dignity remains perpetual.

In addition to the Queen being politically infallible and immortal, her Majesty is also *legally omnipresent;* for as she is considered the *fountain of justice* and general conservator of the peace of the kingdom, she is, in the eyes of the law, supposed always to be present in her various courts of justice. So that when you enter a law court and take your hat off, it is not merely out of respect to the judge or magistrate on the bench, but to the imagined presence of the Queen. Should you or I ever have the misfortune to be committed for contempt of court, we should be punished, not only because we treated with contempt the judge or magistrate, but the Queen, whose representative such judge or magistrate is. The original power of judicature is lodged in society at large, but as justice could not be very well rendered to every one by the people collectively, every nation commits that power to certain select magistrates. In England this authority has immemorially been exercised by the Sovereign, or his or her substitutes, the judges. Our monarchs have, however, delegated for many ages their judicial power to the judges, who, in their several courts, are the depositaries of the fundamental laws of the kingdom, and have a stated jurisdiction regulated by certain and established rules which the Crown itself cannot now alter but by Act of Parliament. And here you must remember that though the Queen is supposed to be present in all her courts of justice, her Majesty cannot personally assume to decide any case, civil or criminal, but must leave such decision to her judges. And when any judicial act is referred to the Queen by any Act of Parliament, it is understood to be done in some court of justice according to the law. So you see that the Queen is not the author of justice, but only the distributor, being, as it were, the steward of the public to dispense it to whom it is due: in fact, her Majesty is not the spring but the reservoir whence right and equity are conducted by a thousand channels to every individual.

You have often seen in the daily papers, among the law intelligence, the Queen *versus*, and then the name of the person prosecuted. Perhaps this has puzzled you, and you cannot make out why her Majesty should appear in the capacity of *prosecutor*. Well, it is very simple. All offences are deemed to be theoretically against either the peace, crown, or dignity of the Queen. And though these offences seem to be rather against the kingdom than the Crown, yet as the public has delegated all its powers with regard to the execution of the laws to one visible magistrate, all affronts to those powers are offences against her Majesty, to whom they are so delegated. Hence the Queen is the proper person to prosecute for all public offences, as she is the one injured in the eye of the law. And for this reason her Majesty has the power to pardon; for it is only fair that the one who is injured should have the power of forgiving.

As her Majesty is what is termed the fountain of justice, so also is she the *fountain of honour*. The Queen of these realms can alone create a peer, baronet, or knight, or confer privileges upon private persons. It is also in the power only of her Majesty to erect corporations, whereby a number of private persons are united together, and enjoy many powers and immunities in their political capacity which otherwise they could not possess. No charter, however, conferring political power or franchise in Great Britain or her colonies, can be granted by the Crown without the concurrence of Parliament.

The Queen is the *head of the army and navy*, and in this capacity has the sole power of raising and regulating fleets and armies; but since 1688 this prerogative has been subjected to such constitutional restraints that it is impossible it can be exercised to the detriment of English liberty.

As her Majesty is head of the army, so is she *head of the Church* established in England. She convenes and dissolves all ecclesiastical synods or convocations, and nominates to vacant bishoprics and certain other ecclesiastical preferments. All appellate authority which, previous to the Reformation, was exercised over members of the Established Church by the Pope, is now vested in the Crown of England, and every ecclesiastical court in England must be held in the name of her Majesty.

By the laws of our land, the Queen is also regarded as the *arbiter* of domestic commerce; but this branch of the royal prerogative is now mainly exercised by the Board of Trade, which is specially charged to superintend all Government measures brought before Parliament relating to trade and commerce. As regards foreign commerce, that is left to the law of merchants.

The Queen, being the *representative of her people*, has the sole power of sending ambassadors to foreign states, and of receiving ambassadors at home. And in her Majesty is vested alone the right of making treaties and alliances, and of declaring war and peace.

Thus, Gentlemen, you see that our gracious Majesty, whom some people wish to make out is a mere state puppet, has some power and authority notwithstanding. Perhaps you say, All very well; but how about Parliament? Cannot Parliament do everything, and make the Queen of no account? Well, let us look into the question a little. But you must remember, when you talk about Parliament, that the Queen herself is a constituent part of the supreme legislative power, and that she has the prerogative of rejecting such provisions in Parliament as she judges improper.

Since the system of Parliamentary government, consequent upon the Revolution of 1688, has become fully developed, the public authority of the Crown in England is only exercised in acts of representation, or through the medium of ministers, who are responsible to Parliament for every public act of her Majesty, as well as for the general policy which they have been called upon to administer. This is termed the theory of royal impersonality, which, from not being properly understood, has given rise to various misrepresentations concerning the true place and position the Queen occupies in the government of the state. Prior to 1688 the government of England was mainly carried on by virtue of the royal prerogative—that is to say, by the king in person, with the advice of his ministers, who were responsible only to their Sovereign for the ordinary conduct of public affairs. This, as you well know, occasioned frequent contests between the Crown and Parliament, which at one time resulted in the horrors of civil war. But the development of the Constitution, effected by the Revolution of 1688, has resulted in the transference of the force of the State from the Crown to the House of Commons. Instead of government by *prerogative*, we have government by *Parliament;* but in all cases the sanction of the Queen is necessary for the passing of any measure. So that the leading principles of the British constitution, as now interpreted, are the personal irresponsibility of the sovereign, the responsibility of ministers, and the inquisitorial power of Parliament.

Now, you often hear it said that the Ministry is the *real* Sovereign of this country, and that to it the whole of the executive power is assigned. This is not the case. Her Majesty retains full discretionary powers for deliberating and determining upon every recommendation which is tendered for her sanction by her ministers; and as every important act of administration must be submitted for the approval of the Crown, her Majesty is enabled to exercise a considerable control over the government of the country. It is true that the Crown seldom refuses to act upon the advice deliberately pressed upon it by its servants; but the power of the Queen to control the measures of her ministers could be exercised at any moment if the exercise became necessary, and was sanctioned by the approbation of the country. Should the Crown ever refuse to accept the advice of its minister, the inevitable consequence to the minister would be the tender of his resignation. But unless the views of the Crown find a response from the nation at large, and are accepted by Parliament, they cannot ultimately prevail, for no policy can be carried out by the government of England but such as meets with the sober approval of Parliament and of the people.

Lord Palmerston said, "It is a fundamental error to suppose that the power of the Crown to reject laws has ceased to exist. . . . That power survives as before, but it is exercised in a different manner. Instead of being exercised upon the laws presented for the royal assent, it is exercised by anticipation in the debates in Parliament. It is delegated to those who are the responsible advisers of the Crown; and it is therefore not possible that a law passed by the two Houses should be presented to the Crown, and should then by the Crown be refused. And why is this? Because it cannot be imagined that a law should have received the consent of both Houses of Parliament, in which the responsible ministers of the Crown are sitting, debating, acting, and voting, unless those who advise the Crown have agreed to that law, and are therefore prepared to counsel the sovereign to assent to it." And on this point Mr Gathorne Hardy says, " Her Majesty has no constitutional right to abdicate that part of her prerogative which entitles her to put a veto upon any measure she thinks fit. . . . Nor is this veto of the English monarch an empty form. It is not difficult to conceive the occasion when, supported by the sympathies of a loyal people, its exercise might defeat an unconstitutional ministry and a corrupt Parliament."

Again, the Queen has the unquestioned power of choosing her responsible ministers; and the continuance of the royal confidence in an existing Ministry is an essential requisite to its remaining in office. Should the Ministry exhibit internal dissensions, or differ from the Sovereign, or from the country at large; or should their measures be ruinous to the interests of the nation, or there exist a general feeling of distrust of them throughout the country, her Majesty can dismiss them. The Houses of Parliament have, it is true, the undeniable right to advise the Queen on this matter; but this right cannot be pressed so far as to render her Majesty accountable to Parliament for her conduct in changing her advisers. All ministers chosen by the Sovereign are entitled to receive from Parliament, if not implicit confidence, at least a fair trial. And that this has been the practice of the Constitution the political student will easily see by examining the questions that arose upon the appointments of Mr Pitt as Prime Minister in 1783, of Mr Addington in 1801, of the Duke of Portland in 1807, of Sir Robert Peel in 1834, and of the late lamented Earl of Derby in 1852, 1858, and in 1866. In all these instances the Prime Ministers were nominated solely by the Sovereign, in the face of a hostile majority in the House of Commons. It is now universally conceded that the Prime Minister should be the *free choice* of the Crown, and this is almost the only act which is the *personal* act of the Sovereign;* yet, as no minister can carry on the government of the country for any length of time who does not possess the confidence of Parliament, this selection is hence practically limited. And as incoming ministers are held responsible to Parliament for the policy which occasioned the retirement of their predecessors in office, ample security is offered that

* "I offered no opinion as to the choice of a successor. That is almost the only act which is the personal act of the sovereign; it is for the sovereign to determine in whom her confidence shall be placed."—*Sir R. Peel on his resignation of office.*

no ministerial changes will be effected by the authority of the Crown but such as commend themselves to the judgment of Parliament. With regard to the appointment of the other members of the Ministry, the Sovereign has no authoritative voice in their selection; that duty is left to the Prime Minister, who chooses his colleagues, and then submits their names for royal approval. Of course, the expression of a strong personal feeling on the part of the Crown has great weight in excluding a person from office or including him—at least for a time. Thus Fox was for a long time excluded from the Cabinet on account of George III.'s dislike to him. In the Ministry of Addington, in 1801, Lord Eldon became Lord Chancellor owing to the wish of George III. Mr Canning was for some time excluded from the Cabinet owing to the dislike of George IV. towards him. In 1828, on the formation of the Wellington Coalition Ministry, George IV. objected to receive Lord Grey into the Cabinet. And in 1835, the late Lord Brougham was not replaced in the office of Lord Chancellor, because he was personally displeasing to William IV. However, all considerations on the part of the Crown must ultimately yield to a regard for the public interests and the Sovereign must

HER RELATIONS WITH THE MINISTRY. 23

be prepared to accept as his or her advisers those selected by the Prime Minister.

Should difficulties occur in the formation of a Ministry, the Queen can send for any peer or privy councillor for advice, whose counsel she might consider serviceable to her in the emergency. Thus, upon the resignation of the Russell Ministry in 1851, her Majesty sent for the Duke of Wellington, not for the purpose of intrusting him with the formation of a Cabinet, but that she might take counsel from him; and again, in 1852, upon the resignation of the Derby Ministry, the Queen sent for the Marquess of Lansdowne for a similar purpose. For all advice, however, so given, the peer or privy councillor is liable to be called to account by Parliament, should such advice be followed by consequences requiring parliamentary interposition. The Ministry once formed, the members of the Administration are formally appointed to their offices by the Queen, at a meeting of the Privy Council held especially for the purpose. They are introduced by the Prime Minister to her Majesty, and then receive the seals of office from the royal hands. It is always in the power of the Crown, acting through its responsible advisers, to dismiss from office a minister of state, and Parliament has no right to interfere in such a case unless this prerogative has been exercised in an arbitrary manner. Thus, in 1795, Earl Fitzwilliam, when Lord-Lieutenant of Ireland, was recalled on account of having favoured a policy with regard to Roman Catholic emancipation which was embarrassing to the Government. The motives of the recall were demanded by Parliament, but the Ministry refused to enter into particulars, as the power of dismissing its servants without assigning any cause was vested in the Crown, and their determination was sustained by large majorities in both Houses of Parliament. The Prime Minister, on account of his being the proper medium of communication between the Sovereign and the Administration, owing to his position as head of the Government and the minister personally selected by the Queen, is bound to inform her Majesty of all events of political importance—such as decisions of Parliament on matters of public concern, and those of the Cabinet on public policy, and to take the royal pleasure thereupon. No important act of Government, committing her Majesty to a particular course, can be performed by ministers without the knowledge and consent of the Queen. Thus, in 1800, Mr Pitt, by neglecting this rule, lost office and his King's confidence; and in our own times, Lord Palmerston, in 1851, was removed from the post of Secretary of State for Foreign Affairs on account of having written and sent to its destination an important despatch without first having submitted it to her Majesty. In minor matters, the ministers have a separate discretion in their several departments. As a proof of the effective control which the Crown exercises over the government of the country, every day despatch-boxes containing official reports, correspondence, &c., are forwarded to her Majesty for the royal approval or signature from the offices of the Principal Secretaries of State, and the Admiralty, and from the Prime Minister. The consideration of these papers forms an important part of the daily routine of the Queen's labours. Till 1862, every separate commission for officers of the army, marines, &c., was signed by her Majesty; but that duty now devolves upon the Commander-in-Chief and a Secretary of State. Should circumstances occur rendering the personal exercise of the royal functions inconvenient or impossible, the powers of the Crown may be delegated to commissioners or other substitutes, provided that a special authority under the royal sign-manual be issued for the purpose. Formerly lords-justices and guardians were appointed for the administration of the government during the absence of the Sovereign from the realm; but owing to royal visits abroad being of so infrequent occurrence, and the facilities afforded by railways, this custom has fallen into desuetude. At least, when her Majesty, in 1843, visited the King of the French, and in 1845 visited Germany, such officers were not appointed.

From one duty which the sovereigns of England had in former times to perform the Queen is exempt. Her Majesty never attends at meetings of the Cabinet, owing to the necessity of the deliberations of the Council being private and confidential. The absence of the Sovereign on these occasions arose from the accidental circumstance of the inability of George I. to express himself in the English language. When formerly the monarch of these realms took an immediate part in the direction of public affairs, no Cabinet Council could be held without his presence; but under the existing system of government through responsible ministers, the absence of the Sovereign during such meetings is in entire conformity with our theory of constitutional government.

Having endeavoured to show the power of her

Majesty over her ministers, let us briefly regard her relations with the Parliament. In the first place, her Majesty is a constituent part of Parliament, as I have already told you—Parliament being composed of the King or Queen, the Lords Spiritual and Temporal, and the Commons. The legal existence of Parliament results altogether from the exercise of the royal prerogative. Her Majesty only has the power of summoning it; it must commence its deliberations at the time appointed by the Queen, and cannot continue them longer than she may allow. There have been only two instances in which the Lords and Commons have met of their own authority—namely, previous to the restoration of Charles II., and at the Revolution in 1688.

There is one contingency upon which the Parliament may meet without summons under the authority of an Act of Parliament. It was provided in the reign of Queen Anne that "in case there should be no Parliament in being at the time of the demise of the Crown, then the last preceding Parliament should immediately convene and sit at Westminster, as if the said Parliament had never been dissolved." By a statute in the reign of George III., a Parliament so revived would only continue in existence for six months, if not sooner dissolved.

Before Parliament can enter upon its duties it must be opened by the personal presence of the Queen, or by her delegated authority. At the beginning of every new Parliament, and of every session after a prorogation, the cause of summons must be declared to both Houses either by her Majesty or by commissioners appointed to represent her, in a speech from the Throne. Till this has been done, neither House can enter upon any business. Since the introduction of the Ministers of the Crown into Parliament, much of the direct authority of the sovereigns of England has been curtailed. The Sovereign is no longer called upon to perform ungracious acts towards his Parliament, or held personally accountable for a policy distasteful to that body. There is now no necessity for invoking the royal veto for the rejection of bills disapproved of by the Crown, because the constitutional influence of the Ministry generally suffices to control their fate. In fact, the royal veto upon bills in Parliament has not been exercised for upwards of 150 years; but, as I have just said, circumstances might arise at any time that would justify the Crown in resorting to such a course.

According to Earl Russell, it is the privilege, and even the duty, of the two Houses of Parliament to advise the Queen upon whatever subject it is her duty to act—a statement fully borne out by Burke, who says it is the privilege of Parliament to interfere by authoritative advice and admonition upon every act of executive government without exception. You must remember here, though, that Parliament is designed for *counsel*, not for rule—for control, and not for *administration*. Mr Canning defined the House of Commons to be a council of control as well as a council of advice; and declared that in cases of adequate importance, especially where the prerogative was concerned, it should endeavour by the timely interposition of advice to prevent the necessity of control. Any *direct* interference by Parliament in the details of government is inconsistent with her Majesty's authority, and a departure from the fundamental principles of the British Constitution. The supreme executive authority belongs to the Crown, nor do the measures adopted by its ministers in the exercise of this authority require the previous sanction of Parliament. Parliament, when complaining of a grievance, or expressing its sense upon some objectionable system of administration, is perfectly competent to approach the Crown by address with advice upon the subject. Thus, in 1836, the House of Commons begged his Majesty to discourage Orange Lodges and secret societies generally, which led to the formal dissolution of the Orange Society of the United Kingdom. Again, in 1856, an address to the Queen for the issue of a commission to determine the site of the New National Gallery was carried against the Ministry, and a commission granted by the Crown. Various other precedents also confirm this point. However, as long as any existing Government retains the confidence of Parliament, it is unwise as a general principle to interfere with it in matters of administration. Should the Crown itself attempt to encroach upon the functions of Parliament, it is the duty of that august body to interpose, and to call to account the Ministry which is responsible for any excess of executive authority. Her Majesty can neither alter, add to, nor dispense with any existing law of the realm; but in times of emergency the Crown, acting under the advice of responsible ministers, may properly anticipate the future action of Parliament by a temporary suspension of certain classes of statutes. Such power is exercised by Orders in Council or Royal Proclamations.

"A large proportion of what may be called the details of legislation rests upon the authority of Orders in Council. . . . As examples of the variety and importance of the subjects to which the form of quasi-legislation is applicable, it may be stated that Orders in Council, or Royal Proclamations* which are usually issued in pursuance of the same, are promulgated for the assembling, prorogation, and dissolution of Parliament; for declaring war; for confirming or disallowing the Acts of Colonial Legislatures; for giving effect to treaties; for extending the terms of patents; for granting charters of incorporation to companies or municipal bodies; for proclaiming ports, fairs, &c.; for deciding causes on appeal; for creating ecclesiastical districts; for granting exemptions from the law of mortmain; for the regulation of the Board of Admiralty, and of appointments to offices in the various departments of state; for creating new offices, and defining the qualifications of persons to fill the same; and for declaring the period at which certain Acts of Parliament (the operation of which has been left by the legislature to the discretion of the Queen in Council) shall be enforced. When the Sovereign declares war

* A Royal Proclamation cannot make a law, but it can add force to a law already made.

against a foreign Power, proclamations are usually issued, materially altering the ordinary laws relating to trade, and imposing rules for the conduct of trade with neutrals or belligerents. Proclamations are also issued to fix the mode, time, and circumstances of putting into execution certain laws, the operation of which has been left to the discretion of the executive government; or, for the purpose of making formal declaration of existing laws and penalties, and of the intention of Government to enforce the same; or, to appoint and direct the keeping of a day of observance, whether as a fast or thanksgiving."

Abstractly, however, the Crown has no *constitutional* right to issue either Orders in Council or Royal Proclamations which appear to sanction any departure from the laws of the land, but trusts to the good sense of the people and to Parliament to indemnify the issuers. And Parliament has always been willing to indemnify the Government for the timely exercise of authority for the public welfare, although it may have led to an overstepping of the constitutional limits of executive power.

Now let us see what control her Majesty has over the public expenditure. No doubt you are all aware, that from a very early period in the history of England the right of taxation, and the granting of supplies for the public service, belong exclusively to Parliament. You know that in Magna Charta it is enacted that "no scutage or aid shall be imposed in our kingdom unless by the general council;" that in the statute *De tallagio non concedendo* it is declared that "no tallage or aid shall be levied without the assent of the archbishop, bishops, earls, barons, knights, burgesses, and other freemen of the land;" that in the Bill of Rights it is guaranteed that " no man be compelled to make any gift, loan, or benevolence or tax, without common consent by Act of Parliament;" and that it is finally established by the Act of Settlement that "money levied for the use of the Crown, without grant of Parliament, is illegal." Thus, then, the Crown is entirely dependent upon Parliament for its revenues; but, though dependent, it has a direct control over all supplies to be raised in the House. The true doctrine on this head has been briefly stated by May, in the following words: " The Crown, acting with the advice of its responsible ministers, being the executive power, is charged with the management of all the revenues of the country, and with all payments for the public service. The Crown, therefore, in the first instance, makes known to the Commons the pecuniary necessities of the Government, and the Commons grant such aids or supplies as are required to satisfy these demands, and provide by taxes, and by the appropriation of other sources of the public income, the ways and means to meet the supplies which are granted by them. Thus the Crown demands money, the Commons grant it, and the Lords assent to the grant. But the Commons do not vote money unless it be required by the Crown; nor impose nor augment taxes unless they be necessary for meeting the supplies which they have voted, or are about to vote, and for supplying general deficiencies in the revenue. The Crown has no concern in the nature or distribution of taxes; but the foundation of all parliamentary taxation is, its necessity for the public service, as declared by the Crown through its constitutional advisers." No money can be voted by Parliament for any purpose whatever except at the demand of the Crown; no petition for any sum of money relating to the public service can be received by Parliament unless recommended by the Crown. Parliament cannot proceed upon any motion for a grant or charge upon the public revenue, whether payable out of the Consolidated Fund or out of moneys to be provided by Parliament, unless recommended from the Crown; and all propositions for the levying of a new tax or duty, or the repeal of an existing impost, must emanate from the ministers of the Crown. On the other hand, Parliament will not permit any person to lend money to the Crown, or to any department of State, for public purposes, without its sanction. All money transactions between the Bank of England and the Treasury, without express parliamentary authority, are forbidden. Advances out of the public funds can only be made by authority of Parliament, except in certain very special cases. The Crown cannot remit any loans or debts due to it by foreign powers, corporations, or individuals, without the consent of Parliament, though the conduct of the Crown in this respect has been occasionally irregular. When a sum of money to which the Crown is entitled is surrendered by a foreign power, it is customary to surrender the same by treaty, which is not contingent upon the assent of Parliament. But when the Crown undertakes to pay a sum of money, such payment is made conditional upon the assent of Parliament.

I daresay many of you remember reading in English history about the conflicts between the King and Parliament respecting the question of granting supplies. Since the introduction of parliamentary government, however, the demands of the Crown for supplies for particular services have seldom been refused. As a general rule, whatever sums are required for the use of the State, the Commons freely grant; though it is always in the power of the House to refuse to grant any particular item until satisfied with the reasons given for it. The House of Commons has the right of withholding altogether the supplies asked for on the part of the Crown; and before the introduction of parliamentary government, as you all well know, this power was often made use of to wrest from an arbitrary monarch the redress of grievances. But now there is no longer any need to resort to such an extreme measure. The precedent of 1784 is the solitary instance since 1688 in which the Commons have exercised their power of delaying the supplies, and then the experiment failed, and has never been repeated.

Though all money matters ought first to receive the sanction of Parliament, yet there are certain occasions when the Crown may be compelled to defray expenses which have not been provided for by Parliament, and hence assume the responsibility of incurring expenditure without the previous knowledge of Parliament. Such was the case when Mr Pitt, at the commencement of the French revolutionary war, advanced upwards of £1,200,000 to

Germany without the knowledge of Parliament; and again in 1859 and 1860, when there had been an excess of expenditure of more than £1,000,000 not voted by Parliament. To meet these unforeseen disbursements, provision is made by means of the "Treasury Chest" and the "Civil Contingencies Fund." The "Treasury Chest" is a fund maintained to supply specie required by the treasury chests in the colonies, and to make the necessary advances for carrying on the public service at the various naval and military stations. This fund is limited to £1,300,000. The "Civil Contingencies Fund" is limited to £120,000, and is for the purpose of defraying unforeseen expenditure for civil services at home. There is also another fund, that for "Secret Services," but the greater part of the amount is annually voted in supply. In former times the taxes which were granted by Parliament were handed over to the King, to be expended by him in maintaining his state, and for keeping up the military and naval services. He had also estates in various parts of the country, called the *crown-lands*, the rents and profits of which were paid into his treasury. The *revenue*, or annual income of the country derived from the taxes imposed by Parliament, and the income from these estates (with the exception of the

Duchy of Lancaster, which belongs to her Majesty, not as Queen of England, but as Duchess of Lancaster) is now collected into one fund called the *Consolidated Fund.* The first charge upon this fund is the payment of interest upon the National Debt called the *Funds,* and upon the *unfunded debt.*

The next charge is an allowance called the *Civil List,* apportioned to the Queen for the support of her household and the dignity of her crown. This was fixed by statute at £385,000, to be paid annually, and to be appropriated as follows: Her Majesty's privy purse, £60,000; salaries of her Majesty's Household, and retired allowances, £131,000; expenses of the household, £172,500; royal bounty and special services, £13,200; pensions, £12,000; and miscellaneous, £8040. On the Consolidated Fund are likewise charged various sums allowed to members of the royal family. The sum for carrying on the civil government, including the salaries of the Ministers of State, judges, and others, is also charged upon the Consolidated Fund, the remainder of which is paid into the Exchequer, for the public service, to defray the expenses of our army, navy, civil service, &c.

I have said that all naval and military authority

is centred in the Sovereign, but subject to such constitutional restraints that it cannot be exercised to the detriment of English liberty. By the Bill of Rights it is expressly enacted "that the raising or keeping a standing army within the kingdom, unless it be with consent of Parliament, is against law." This consent to the continual existence of a standing army is given only for the period of one year at a time by a resolution of the House of Commons. By modern practice, the numbers of men to be employed in the army and navy are annually fixed by resolutions in Committee of Supply, and afterwards included in respect to the army in the Mutiny Act, and in respect to the navy in the Act of Appropriation. It is a direct infringement of the constitution for the Crown to raise more men for the land and sea forces than have been voted by Parliament; but upon occasions of great emergency the Government have assumed the responsibility of increasing the army or navy beyond the numbers actually voted, and have afterwards applied to Parliament to make good the deficiency in the supplies granted for this service. The constitutional security against the abuse of the royal prerogative in the direction and control of our forces lies in the general responsibility of ministers, and the necessity for the sanction of Parliament to the continued existence of the army and navy, by the annual appropriations for the support of these services, and the annual renewal of the Mutiny Acts. Parliament has the full right of interfering in all cases of abuse; of inquiring into the causes of disasters befalling our arms in war; and of advising upon all general questions affecting the wellbeing and efficiency of the army and navy. The Crown has the power, through a responsible minister, of dismissing any of its officers from the army or navy at its own discretion, and without assigning any reason for the Act. In fact, this power is so absolute that even if an officer is acquitted by a court of inquiry, the Crown is justified in removing him from office, upon the advice of a minister responsible to Parliament. In cases of insurrection or rebellion, the Crown is entitled to proclaim martial law when the ordinary authorities are unable to quell disturbances. This power being invoked by the Sovereign, or her representative in any colony or district within the realm, the ordinary laws are therein suspended for a time, and an absolute discretion is vested in the military authorities with regard to their proceedings for the restoration of peace and good order. Ministers of the Crown, however (through whose instrumentality resort should be had under any circumstances to martial law), are responsible to Parliament for their conduct, and must be able to justify their acts under penalty of impeachment or removal from office. Thus in 1865, as you well know, Governor Eyre was removed from office, owing to his having been censured by a Royal Commission for permitting unjustifiable severity whilst suppressing an insurrection in the island of Jamaica, when under martial law.

I now come to the power of the Sovereign with regard to the right of declaring war and making peace. This power is vested exclusively in the Crown, but, like all other prerogatives, must be exercised by the advice and under the responsibility of ministers who are accountable to Parliament, and are liable to impeachment for the improper conduct of a war. The consent of Parliament is not formally required by the constitution, either to the commencement of a war or the conclusion of a peace; but as Parliament furnishes all supplies, and controls the numbers of our army and navy, it becomes difficult for this prerogative to be improperly used. If hostilities about to be entered into are likely to involve serious consequences, it is the duty of ministers to ask for the advice and co-operation of

Parliament in carrying on the war. Parliament is, however, at perfect liberty to offer advice unfavourable to the Ministry, and to refuse its assistance. Thus, in 1782, the American war was brought to a close, contrary to the wishes and intentions of George III., by the interposition of the House of Commons. In 1791, Mr Pitt had to abandon an intended war with Russia, owing to the adverse opinions of the House of Commons; and in 1857, the House of Commons condemned the policy of the war with China, which occasioned a dissolution of Parliament, though the result of such condemnation was in favour of the Ministry. However, with regard to this liberty of Parliament, it appears that if the Government enter upon a foreign war in defence of the honour or interests of the State, it is the duty of Parliament to afford the Crown an adequate support; for in 1854, upon the declaration of the war with Russia, Mr Disraeli said—" If her Majesty informs us that she has found it necessary to engage in war, I hold that it is not an occasion when we are to enter into the policy or impolicy of the advice by which her Majesty has been guided. It is our duty to rally round the throne, and on a subsequent occasion to question the policy of the Ministry."

And now, Gentlemen, I come to the last act of

the royal prerogative which I intend discussing in my lecture to-night—the power of the Crown with regard to foreign affairs. And, firstly, her Majesty is the constitutional representative of the nation in its intercourse with foreign powers. The medium of communication between the Queen and the representatives of foreign nations is the Secretary of State for Foreign Affairs, whose duty it is to convey the opinions and conclusions of the Government upon matters arising out of the relations of the British Crown with other countries. Parliament has to be informed from time to time of everything which is necessary to explain the policy of the Government, in order that it may interpose with advice or remonstrance. Of course, a certain amount of discretion is always allowed to the Government in communicating or withholding documents asked for by Parliament. Occasionally the Government have laid before Parliament papers in regard to disputes still pending, but this is only in especial cases; Parliament has, however, no right to dictate the answers to such disputes. Private and confidential correspondence, and autograph letters from sovereign princes to her Majesty, are not communicated to Parliament. The Queen, as representative of her people, has, as I have already said, the exclusive right of sending ambassadors to foreign States, and of receiving ambassadors at home. This prerogative is unquestionable, and should not be interfered with by either House of Parliament, except in cases of manifest corruption or abuse. It would be a breach of this prerogative for either House of Parliament to communicate directly with any foreign power: all such communications must be made officially through the Government, and by a responsible minister of the Crown.

Secondly, it is the peculiar function of her Majesty to make treaties and alliances with foreign states, acting under the advice of her responsible ministers. The sanction or ratification by Parliament of any treaty is not necessary to constitute its validity. Parliament has, however, the right of withholding its sanction to those parts of a treaty requiring a legislative enactment to give it force, or to impeach the ministers of the Crown, who are responsible for the treaty if it disapproves of the measure. Our history contains numerous instances of the censure by Parliament of ministers of the Crown for misconduct of public affairs. Thus, in 1451 the Earl of Suffolk was impeached for making a peace without the assent of the Privy Council;

in 1529, among the articles against Wolsey were charges of carrying on diplomatic correspondence without the King's knowledge; in 1701 the Earl of Oxford was impeached by the Commons for advising treaties for dividing the dominions of Spain, &c. Parliament has, however, no power to change or modify in any way a treaty itself. With regard to pending negotiations, if Parliament be satisfied with the general principles upon which such negotiations are being conducted, and approve of the general policy of the Government, it should abstain from all interference. Papers regarding pending negotiations with foreign powers are only communicated to Parliament at the discretion of the Crown. When the *result* of the negotiations conducted by ministers has been communicated to Parliament, it is the duty of both Houses to support or condemn those negotiations as they may deem the interests of the nation require.

And now, lastly, let us look at the Crown's power of interfering with the internal concerns of foreign nations. This power, whenever occasion requires it, is always exercised by her Majesty, acting through the Secretary of State for Foreign Affairs. Great delicacy, however, is always necessary in all acts of intervention lest they should irritate instead of conciliate. Direct interference by Parliament in the domestic concerns of a foreign country would be highly unconstitutional. Should the Crown possess a distinct ground for interposition in a domestic matter within a foreign territory, Parliament can address her Majesty to exercise that right; but if the Ministry, on the grounds of political expediency, oppose such address, it should not be persevered in. Thus, in 1836 the House of Commons moved an address to King William IV. to intercede with the King of the French for the release of Prince Polignac and other state prisoners confined in prison; but Lord Palmerston, then Foreign Secretary, declared such a step inexpedient, and the motion was withdrawn. But in 1832 and 1842 the Ministry acquiesced in motions made in the House of Commons for addresses for copies of ukases issued by Russia relating to the administration of Poland, because England had been party to a treaty in 1815 by which the condition of Poland had been regulated, and Russia had acted in contravention to that treaty.

During the present reign, three points, hitherto undetermined, have been decided by constitutional authority. The first is the right of her Majesty to employ a Private Secretary. Until 1805 no English monarch ever required the services of a Private Secretary, but George III., owing to failure of sight, employed one for the first time—a precedent which was followed by George IV., William IV., and our gracious Queen. This appointment has been opposed as unconstitutional, because it allows the secrets of the Cabinet to pass through a third person, and thus subjects the advice of ministers to their sovereign to the revision of his private secretary. Such appointment is, however, now justifiable, owing to the increasing amount of routine duty devolving upon an English Sovereign at the present day.* The second point is, that the great offices

---

* The 'Saturday Review,' in an article on the death of General Grey, her Majesty's late Private Secretary, remarks: " The Private Secretary of the Queen has to lead a very laborious life, for the simple reason that the life of the Sovereign he serves is necessarily very laborious. He has the reward of doing really good work, and of doing it under the eyes of a person who can appreciate what he does. He has also the reward of exercising an important but very indirect influence over the course of public affairs. But it is a great mistake to suppose that the Queen's Private Secretary has power in the shape of commanding patronage, or of influencing the mind of the Sovereign on questions where the head of the Ministry is brought into direct contact with the Queen. What amount of influence he has will depend upon, not only on the man himself, but on the accidental circumstances in which he may find himself. The Queen has an enormous amount of daily business to go through. . . . Every-

of the Court, and situations in the Household held by members of Parliament, should be included in the political arrangements made on a change of the Administration. The offices of Mistress of the Robes and Ladies of the Bed-Chamber, when held by ladies connected with the outgoing ministers, are resigned on a change of Ministry. And the third point is, that for the first time the constitutional position of a Prince-Consort has been defined as "the confidential adviser and assistant of a female sovereign."

And now, Gentlemen, I here conclude. Within the brief limits of a lecture I do not pretend to have exhausted my subject, but I have endeavoured to pass under review the duties and principal prerogatives of her Majesty, and the proper functions of Parliament in relation to them. I have endeavoured to show you that the supreme executive

thing that is done in every department is made known to her, and her pleasure taken upon it. Much of the departmental business is, of course, mere routine, and the Queen has not really to keep a watch over it. But every important question arising in every department has to be brought before her, and in some departments the Sovereign has always taken an especial interest. Everything connected with the troops and with the fleet is watched with the utmost vigilance by the Sovereign, and it is a part of the traditions of English Royalty not to relax this vigilance."

authority of the State in all matters, civil and military, together with jurisdiction and supremacy over all causes and persons ecclesiastical in the realm, belongs to her Majesty by virtue of her queenly office. I have said that she is the fountain of all State authority, dignity, and honour, and the source of all political jurisdiction; that she is the head of the Imperial Legislature, which derives its existence from the Crown; and that it is her Majesty's especial prerogative to declare war and make peace, and also to contract alliances with foreign nations. But still I have left much unsaid, for volumes might be written upon the subject; but if in my lecture to-night I have proved to you that the Queen of these realms holds a real and not a nominal office—that she is a substantive power in our mixed constitution, and not a State puppet in the hands of her ministers—my object in coming among you has been attained.

GOD SAVE THE QUEEN!

LECTURE II.

THE MINISTRY.

> "A patriot both the king and country serves,
> Prerogative and privilege preserves;
> Of each our laws the certain limit show,
> One must not ebb, nor th' other overflow;
> Betwixt the Prince and Parliament we stand,
> The barriers of the State on either hand:
> May neither overflow, for then they drown the land."
> —DRYDEN.

"The patriot aims at his private good in the public: the knave makes the public subservient to his private interest. The former considers himself as part of a whole, the latter considers himself as the whole."

"A man who hath no sense of God or conscience, would you make such a one guardian to your child? If not, why guardian to the State?"

"When the heart is right there is true patriotism."—BISHOP BERKELEY, *Maxims concerning Patriotism.*

GENTLEMEN,—As in my last lecture to you I stated that much of the power which formerly belonged to English sovereigns had, owing to the development of the system of parliamentary government, been delegated to the hands of resposible ministers, I shall to-night try to explain to you who those ministers are, what offices they control, and what is their exact constitutional position; and in order to facilitate this explanation, I shall divide my subject into three heads.

 I. The Ministers who are Privy Councillors *ex officio*.
 II. The Ministers who belong to that select committee of the Privy Council which we call the "Cabinet Council;" and
 III. The Ministers who are not Privy Councillors.

Firstly.—Ever since the introduction of monarchial institutions into Britain, the Sovereign has always been surrounded by a select band of confidential advisers to assist him or her in the government of the country. At no time could the Sovereign act according to law, without advice, in the public concerns of the kingdom. The institution of the Crown of England and the institution of the Privy Council are coeval—that is to say, the one never existed without the other. At the era of the Norman Conquest, the King's Council, or, as we now call it, the Privy Council, was composed of certain select persons of the nobility and great officers of state, specially summoned by the royal command, and with whom the King usually advised in matters of state and government. At first the King's councillors, as confidential servants of the Crown, were present at every meeting of the High Court of Parliament, to advise upon matters judicial in the House of Lords; but in the reign of Richard II. the Privy Council dissolved its judicial connection with the Lords, and assumed an independent jurisdiction of its own. To trace to you the rise and fall of the power of the Privy Council would be beyond the object of my lecture; suffice it to say, that in the earlier stages of our history the Council, with a vigorous prince on the throne, became the mere instrument of his will; and at other times its influence was exerted to curb the arbitrary exercise of kingly rule, and to aggrandise the authority of the ministers. The King's councillors were privileged to approach the Sovereign with advice or remonstrance upon any matter affecting the common weal. Through the instrumentality of the Chancellor they could refuse to give effect to the King's wishes or to legalise his grant, for from a very early period they had claimed to take cognisance of every grant or writ issued by the King; and as the Great Seal was always in the custody of the Chancellor, it could not be affixed to any document except by his hand. The business before the Council was an extraordinary combination of the executive and legislative functions of the Government—grave affairs of state and questions of domestic and foreign policy, the preservation of the King's peace, the management of the finances, the affairs of aliens, the regulation of trade, the settlement of ecclesiastical disputes, and numerous other duties, appear to have formed part of its ordinary administrative labours. It was in the reign of Henry VI. that the King's Council first assumed the name of the "Privy Council," and it was also during the minority of this King that a select Council was gradually emerging from out of the larger body of the Privy Council, which ultimately resulted in the institution of our modern Cabinet. From the accession of Henry VII. to the reign of Charles I. the Privy Council was wholly subservient to the royal will, and the instrument of unconstitutional and arbitrary proceedings. The first act of the Long Parliament was to deprive the Council of most of its judicial power, leaving, however, its constitution and political functions unchanged. Since the Revolution of 1688 the Privy Council has dwindled into comparative insignificance, when contrasted with its original authoritative position. Its judicial functions are now restrained within very narrow limits. The only relic of its ancient authority in criminal matters is its power of taking examinations, and issuing commitments for treason. It still, however, continues to exercise an original jurisdiction in advising the Crown concerning the grant of charters, and it has exclusively assumed the appellate jurisdiction over the colonies and dependencies of the Crown, which formerly appertained to the Council in Parliament Theoretically, the Privy Council still retains its ancient supremacy, and in a constitutional point of view is presumed to be the only legal and responsible Council of the Crown.

Though, as I have just said, most of the high and important powers of the Privy Council have been curtailed, yet it still possesses no inconsiderable amount of its original functions, both in the prosecution of public inquiries, and also in the discharge of special administrative duties. As her Majesty can only act through her privy councillors, or upon their advice, all the higher and more formal acts of administration must proceed from the authority of the Sovereign in Council, and their performance be directed by orders issued by the Sovereign at a meeting of the Privy Council specially convened for that purpose. No rule can be laid down defining those political acts of the Crown which may be performed upon the advice of particular ministers, or those which must be exercised only "in Council"—the distinction depends partly on usage and partly on the wording of Acts of Parliament. The subjects generally disposed of by the authority of an Order in Council I have already specified to you in my lecture on the 'Queen.'* The law officers of the Crown are also invariably consulted upon such Orders, and are responsible for their legality. When the matter to be determined in Council relates to a mere question of administration—such as the creation of additional secretaries of state from time to time, and the appointment of the necessary establishments for the new departments — it is usual for a declaration of the Queen in Council to be made thereupon. Again, all declarations of, or public engagements by, the Sovereign, all consents to marriages by members of the royal family, all appointments of sheriffs for England and Wales, and the like, are made by the Queen in Council. The ancient functions of the Privy Council are now performed by committees, excepting those formal

* See p. 31.

measures which proceed from the authority of her Majesty in Council. The acts of these committees are designated as those of the Lords of the Council. These Lords of Council (who are usually selected by the Lord President of the Council, of whom more hereafter) constitute a high court of record for the investigation of all offences against the Government, and of such other extraordinary matters as may be brought before them. It is competent for the Queen in Council to receive petitions and appeals from India and the colonies, and to refer these or any other matter whatever to the consideration of a committee of the Privy Council, upon whose report the decision of the Sovereign in Council is pronounced. If the matter be one properly cognisable by a legal tribunal, it is referred to the Judicial Committee of the Privy Council. This committee, which is composed of the Lord President, the Lord Chancellor, and such members of the Privy Council as from time to time hold certain high judicial offices, has jurisdiction in appeals from all colonial courts: it is also the supreme court of maritime jurisdiction, and the tribunal wherein the Crown exercises its judicial supremacy in ecclesiastical cases. The Privy Council has also to direct local authorities throughout the kingdom in matters affecting the preservation of the public health. A committee of the Privy Council is also appointed to provide " for the general management and superintendence of Education," and subject to this committee is the Science and Art Department for the United Kingdom. There is also another important committee of the Privy Council which performs administrative functions as a distinct department of government, and that is the committee of her Majesty's Privy Council appointed for the consideration of matters relating to Trade and Foreign Plantations.

Such, briefly, are the chief functions of the Privy Council in these days. Formerly meetings of the Council were frequently held, but they now seldom occur oftener than once in three or four weeks, and are always convened to assemble at the royal residence for the time being. The attendance of seven Privy Councillors used to be regarded as the quorum necessary to constitute a Council for ordinary purposes of state, but this number has been diminished frequently to only three. No Privy Councillor presumes to attend upon any meeting of the Privy Council unless specially summoned. The last time the *whole* Council was convoked was in 1839.

Privy Councillors are appointed absolutely, without patent or grant, at the discretion of the Sovereign. Their number is unlimited, and they may be dismissed, or the whole Council dissolved, at the royal pleasure. No qualification is necessary in a Privy Councillor except that he be a natural-born subject of Great Britain, and even this disability may be removed by special Act of Parliament, as in the cases of the late Prince-Consort and the late King of the Belgians. On the accession of a new Sovereign, the Privy Councillors of the preceding reign are resworn.

The ancient oath of office which Privy Councillors had to take was as follows :—" 1. To advise the Sovereign according to the best of their cunning and discretion. 2. To advise for the Sovereign's honour and good of the public; without partiality through affection, love, meed, doubt, or dread. 3. To keep the Sovereign's counsel secret. 4. To avoid corruption. 5. To help and strengthen the execution of what shall be resolved. 6. To withstand all persons who would attempt the contrary. 7. To observe, keep, and do all that a true and good councillor ought to do to his Sovereign." The following declaration embodies the substance of the oath now in force :—" You shall solemnly and sincerely declare that you will be a true and faithful servant unto her Majesty Queen Victoria as one of her Majesty's Privy Council; you shall keep secret all matters committed and revealed unto you, or that shall be secretly treated of in Council, and generally in all things you shall do as a faithful and true servant ought to do to her Majesty."

This obligation of secrecy is a great constitutional principle, for it is of the greatest importance that there should be entire freedom in the confidential intercourse between the Crown and its advisers. Without the express permission of her Majesty, nothing that has passed between the Queen and her Ministers in their confidential relations with each other can be disclosed to Parliament or to any other body. And this permission would only be granted for state purposes, so as to enable a minister to explain and justify to Parliament his political conduct.

Since the separate existence of the Cabinet Council, meetings of the Privy Council for purposes of deliberation have ceased to be held.

The Privy Council consists ordinarily of the members of the Royal Family, the Archbishops of Canterbury and York, the Bishop of London, all the Cabinet Ministers, the Lord Chancellor, the chief officers of the Royal Household, the Judges of the Courts of Equity, the Chief Justices of the Courts of Common Law, and some of the Puisne Judges, the Ecclesiastical and Admiralty Judges, and the Judge-Advocate, the Lord-Lieutenant of Ireland, the Speaker of the House of Commons, the Ambassadors and the Chief Ministers Plenipotentiary, the Governors of the chief colonies, the Commander-in-Chief, the Vice-President of the Committee of Council for Education, certain other officials I need not particularise, and occasionally a Junior Lord of the Admiralty, though it is not usual for Under Secretaries of State or Junior Lords of the Treasury or Admiralty to have this rank conferred upon them. A seat in the Privy Council is sometimes given to persons retiring from the public service, who have filled responsible situations under the Crown, as an honorary distinction. A Privy Councillor is styled Right Honourable, and he takes precedence of all baronets, knights, and younger sons of viscounts and barons.

Now having thus briefly sketched the history and duties of the Privy Council, I shall proceed to tell you what members of the Privy Council, not being Cabinet Ministers, constitute the Ministry; and here we find the following:—

The Lord-Lieutenant of Ireland.
The Chief Secretary for Ireland.
The Judge-Advocate General.
The Vice-President of the Council for Education; and
The Chief Officers of the Royal Household.

The government of Ireland is formally intrusted to the Queen's Viceroy, usually called the Lord-Lieutenant, but whose official designation is the Lord-Lieutenant General and General Governor of Ireland. This high officer represents the person of her Majesty in Ireland. He is commissioned to keep the peace, the laws and customs of Ireland, to govern the Irish people, to chasten and correct offenders, and to encourage such as do well. He is placed in supreme authority, and has power to pardon criminals or to commute their sentences. The police is subject to his entire control, and he can issue such orders as he thinks necessary to the officers commanding the troops in Ireland. He has almost the entire disposal of all Crown patronage in Ireland, and the right of filling up numerous subordinate posts. No complaint concerning Ireland can be made to her Majesty, unless it has first been brought before the Lord-Lieutenant. In fact, no other subject of the Queen is vested with so extensive regal powers, except perhaps the Viceroy of India. Notwithstanding his power, however, he has to act under the Ministry for the time being, and the Cabinet minister who is ordinarily responsible for advising the Lord-Lieutenant is the Home Secretary, but in matters of moment the Prime Minister interposes his authority. In carrying on the executive government of Ireland, the Lord-Lieutenant is assisted by an Irish Privy Council, consisting of about sixty members, whose sanction is necessary to give validity to many of his official acts. His great officers of state are the Chief Secretary, the Lord Chancellor, the Attorney and Solicitor Generals, and the permanent Under-Secretary, who all (of course, excepting the permanent Under-Secretary) vacate their offices on a change of administration. The Chief Secretary is the Prime Minister of the Lord-Lieutenant, whose duty it is to see that the commands of the Lord-Lieutenant in keeping the peace and the laws of Ireland are fulfilled. He is generally a member of the House of Commons, and sometimes a Cabinet minister.* The duties of

---

* In the present Gladstone Ministry the Chief Secretary for Ireland is a Cabinet minister, though, in the opinion of Sir Robert Peel, grave objections exist to this dignity being conferred on such an official, "as it not only disturbs the relations of a chief

the other officers resemble those of the similar appointments in England.

The Judge-Advocate General presides over the judicial department of the army, and is the sole representative of the Government in all military proceedings before general courts-martial. He prosecutes either in person or by deputy in the Queen's name, and all matters arising out of the administration of martial law come under his supervision. He has no absolute judicial authority, nor any voice in the sentence of the court; but after the trial the case is transmitted to the Horse Guards, and thence to the Judge-Advocate General, who then examines into the sentence, and advises her Majesty as to its confirmation or rejection. This done, the proceedings are returned to the Commander-in-Chief. The Judge-Advocate has usually a seat in the House of Commons, where he acts as the legal adviser of the Government on military questions.* The permanent and working officer of his department is the Deputy Judge-Advocate.

to his subordinate (the Lord-Lieutenant never being included among the Cabinet councillors), but directly inverts those relations, and encourages the Chief Secretary still more to assume for himself the exercise of independent powers."

* It is intended to amalgamate the office of the Paymaster-General with that of the Judge-Advocate.

The Vice-President of the Education Committee *
(which is a Committee of the Privy Council, composed usually of Cabinet ministers, with authority to provide for the general management and superintendence of education, regulated by various Minutes of Council) transacts the current business of the Education Department. The authorising of building grants, and the general distribution of the Educational grant as at present settled by Parliament, is exclusively managed by this officer. The Vice-President is not a responsible official, but has to act in obedience to the Lord President of the Privy Council and the Committee. He is sworn a Privy Councillor in order to attend the meetings of the Education Committee. Until 1867 there was a Vice-President of the Board of Trade, who was a Privy Councillor and a member of the Administration, but this office is now abolished.

The chief officers of the Royal Household are the Lord Steward of the Household, the Lord and Vice Chamberlains, the Master of the Horse, the Treasurer and Comptroller of the Household, the Captain of the corps of Gentlemen-at-Arms, the Captain of the Yeomen of the Guard, the Master of the Buck-

---

* The present Vice-President has been made a Cabinet minister, but it is a most unusual proceeding.

hounds, the Chief Equerry and Clerk Marshal, and the Lords-in-waiting. These offices are for the most part usually held by peers or members of the House of Commons who are the political adherents of the existing Ministry. To describe the duties of these officers would extend my lecture beyond its proposed limits.

I now come to my *second* heading—the ministers belonging to the Cabinet Council, and who constitute the chief members of an Administration. I was obliged to defer describing their duties till now, because without saying something of the Privy Council I could not have mentioned the Cabinet, as the Cabinet is an unrecognised select committee of the Privy Council. The practice of consulting a few confidential advisers instead of the whole Privy Council has been resorted to by English Sovereigns from a very early period; but the first mention of the term *Cabinet* Council, in contradistinction to *Privy* Council, occurs in the reign of Charles I., when the burden of state affairs was intrusted to the Committee of State, which Clarendon says was enviously called the "Cabinet Council." This form of government was at first extremely unpopular, and it was not till 1783 that the Cabinet Council was regulated by those rules which it now enforces, and

E

which are essential to its wellbeing. Before that date the Cabinets were often composed of men of different judgment and principles, and who seldom were of one mind in matters of importance. William III. attempted the first successful reform (Sir W. Temple's scheme was a failure) in the Cabinet, by constructing a Ministry whose members should be of accord upon the general principles of state policy, and be willing to act in unison in their places in Parliament. Before this reformation, the introduction of the King's ministers into Parliament, for the purpose of representing the Crown in the conduct of public business within its walls, was a thing unknown in England. True, that from an early period various ministers had obtained seats in the House of Commons, but they occupied no recognised position, and it was often a mooted point whether they were entitled to sit at all in the House. It was not till the formation of the first parliamentary Ministry by William III. that ministers of the Crown were cordially received by the Commons. "Under the Plantagenets, Tudors, and Stuarts there had been ministers, but no Ministry. The servants of the Crown were not, as now, bound in frank pledge for each other. They were not expected to be of the same opinion even on questions of the gravest importance. Often they were politically and personally hostile to each other, and made no secret of their hostility." It was not long before the nation began to appreciate the advantages of having Cabinet ministers in the legislature to explain and defend the measures and policy of the executive government. But more than a century had to elapse before political unanimity in the Cabinet was recognised as a political maxim. From the first parliamentary Ministry of William III. until the rise of the second William Pitt in 1783 (with the exceptions of the anarchy that existed from 1699 to 1705, when there was no Ministry, and the political agreement during the Ministry of Robert Walpole), divisions in the Cabinet were constantly occurring. At the same council-board were Whigs and Tories, men who advocated High-Church principles and men who favoured Dissent; and it was no uncommon thing to see colleagues in office opposing one another in Parliament upon measures that ought to have been supported by a united Cabinet. In 1812 an attempt was made to form a Ministry consisting of men of opposite political principles, who were invited to accept office not avowedly as a coalition government, but with an offer to the Whig leaders that their friends should be allowed a majority of one in the Cabinet. This offer was declined on the plea that to construct a Cabinet on "a system of counteraction was inconsistent with the prosecution of any uniform and beneficial course of policy." And from that time it has been an established principle that all Cabinets are to be constructed on some basis of political union agreed upon by the members composing the same, when they accept office together. It is also distinctly understood that the members of a Cabinet are jointly and severally responsible for each other's acts, and that any attempt to separate between a particular minister and his colleagues in such matters is unfair and unconstitutional. On the resignation of the Prime Minister in deference to an adverse vote of the House of Commons, all his colleagues also now resign. It was not always so. From 1688 to George I. changes in the Ministry were always gradual, and there is no instance of the simultaneous dismissal of a whole Ministry and their replacement by another till the accession of George I. to the throne, who effected a total change in all the chief officers of state, though this change was due to his dislike to the ministers of Queen Anne, and not on account of prevailing opinions in Parliament. The resignation of Sir Robert Walpole is the first instance of the resignation of a Prime Minister in deference to an adverse vote of the Commons; and the resignation of the Ministry of Lord North is the first instance of a simultaneous change of the whole Administration (excepting Lord Chancellor Thurlow) in deference to the opinions of the House of Commons. From that time, when a change of Ministry has occurred it has been invariably simultaneous and complete. If upon the retirement of a Cabinet any ministers have remained in office, they have been obliged to make a fresh agreement with the incoming Prime Minister before forming part of the new Administration.

Soon after the resignation of Lord North's Ministry, another event occurred which has ever since been regarded as an important precedent in the relation of the King's Council to Parliament—viz., the first instance (after the practice of changing the whole Cabinet at once had been established) of an appeal by the Ministry to the nation at large to reverse the preponderance of parties in Parliament. In 1784 the King resolved to dismiss his ministers, who were personally obnoxious to him, although they were supported by a majority of the House of Commons, and he called Mr Pitt to his counsels.

The House of Commons passed resolutions adverse to his Ministry, and addressed the Crown for his removal. Instead of resigning, Mr Pitt advised the King to dissolve Parliament, and in the new Parliament procured a large majority in his favour. "The precedent of 1784," says Earl Russell, "therefore establishes this rule of conduct—that if the ministers chosen by the Crown do not possess the confidence of the House of Commons, they may advise an appeal to the people, with whom rests the ultimate decision." And this course has been followed on different occasions.

Such, briefly, is a sketch of the rise and development of the Cabinet. The powers of this council have now attained to maturity, and in its hands is placed the entire administration of the foreign and domestic affairs of this kingdom. But though universally recognised as an essential part of our polity, it has no legal existence, and is a body unrecognised by Act of Parliament. The names of those persons who comprise the Cabinet are never officially communicated to the public. The London Gazette simply states that her Majesty has been pleased to appoint certain privy councillors to fill certain high offices in the State, and the fact that they have been called to seats in the Cabinet is not formally promulgated. The numbers of those constituting this council are indefinite, for the statesman constructing a Ministry can put as many persons as he pleases into it, with his Sovereign's consent. The first Cabinet of George I. consisted of eight members; in 1760, the Cabinet consisted of fourteen members; in 1770, of only seven; in 1782, of ten; and in 1783, of eleven. After the death of Mr Pitt, the Cabinet generally consisted of from ten to sixteen persons. At the present time it comprises about fifteen members belonging to the more eminent portion of the Administration. Formerly the Lord Chief Justice of the King's Bench, the Archbishop of Canterbury, the Master of the Mint, and the Commander-in-chief, were included in the Cabinet, but they are now excluded. Occasionally statesmen of high character and experience have seats in a Cabinet without taking any office, as was the case with Earl Fitzwilliam in 1807, with the Marquess of Camden in 1812, with the Earl of Mulgrave in 1820, with the Marquess of Lansdowne and Lord John Russell in 1854, with Lord John Russell again in 1855 and 1856, and with various other statesmen at different times. The members who, *ex-officio*, compose a Cabinet, are—

The Prime Minister, or First Lord of the Treasury.
The Lord High Chancellor.
The Lord President of the Council.
The Lord Privy Seal.
The Chancellor of the Exchequer.
The Secretary of State for the Home Department.
    Do. do. for Foreign Affairs.
    Do. do. of the Colonies.
    Do. do. for War.
    Do. do. for India.
The First Lord of the Admiralty.
The President of the Board of Trade.

Usually, but not invariably, {
 The Chancellor of the Duchy of Lancaster.
 The First Commissioner of Works.
 The President of the Poor Law Board.
 The Postmaster-General.
}

Like the Cabinet Council, the office of Prime Minister is unknown to the law and the constitution. Legally and constitutionally, no one Privy Councillor has, as such, any superiority over another. The Prime Minister is simply the member of the Cabinet who possesses pre-eminently the confidence of the Crown, and to whom the Sovereign thinks fit to intrust the chief direction of the Government. The choice of a Premier, however, is only a matter of private understanding, as there is no express appointment of any member of the Administration to be the Prime Minister. Before 1688 the Prime Minister was the favourite of the King, and his rise and fall depended solely on his royal master's goodwill; but since the development of this office, consequent upon the introduction of parliamentary government, the Premier is now the acknowledged head of a responsible Administration, whose tenure of office mainly depends upon his ability to obtain parliamentary support. It was in the person of Sir Robert Walpole that the office of Prime Minister first began to assume importance, but it will be beyond the scope of these lectures to sketch to you those different stages in the growth of this office which have finally resulted in the supremacy of the First Minister under parliamentary government.

The Prime Minister may be either a peer or a commoner, and his appointment is a personal and not an official distinction. Lord Rockingham in 1765, the Duke of Portland in 1782, and Mr Addington in 1812, had held no office when they were first made Prime Ministers. Lord Bute became Prime Minister before he had ever spoken in Parliament, and Mr Pitt was Premier before he was twenty-four. Usually the Prime Minister holds the office of First Lord of the Treasury, either alone or in connection with that of Chancellor of the Exchequer. Before 1806 the Premiership was occasionally held in connection with different other offices, such as the Secretaryship of State, Lord Privy Seal, and the like, but it is now invariably associated with the office of First Lord of the Treasury. The Treasury, as you well know, is the most important department of the Executive Government, and consists of a board of five members—the First Lord of the Treasury, the Chancellor of the Exchequer, and three Junior Lords—who are officially known as "the Lords Commissioners for executing the office of Lord High Treasurer." The last Lord High Treasurer was the Duke of Shrewsbury in 1714. The First Lord of the Treasury, as head of the Government, occupies a position of great dignity and authority. He does not confine himself to the departmental business of the Treasury, but is cognisant of all matters of real importance that take place in the different departments, so as to be able to exercise a controlling influence in the Cabinet. He is the medium of intercourse between the Cabinet and the Sovereign, and has to conduct all official communications which may be necessary between her Majesty and her responsible advisers. He is expected to be present almost continually in Parliament during the session to explain and defend the policy of the Government, and to guide the deliberations of the Legislature. He is virtually responsible for the disposal of the entire patronage of the Crown. He recommends to the Queen all appointments to vacant archbishoprics, bishoprics, and deaneries of the Established Church, and to all the church livings belonging to the Crown which are not in the gift of the Lord Chancellor. The Premier virtually selects all his colleagues in the Ministry, and it is upon his recommendation that new peers are created, and other distinguished honours conferred by the Crown. Though he meets his colleagues in the Cabinet Councils upon a footing of perfect equality, yet he possesses a degree of weight and authority which is not shared by any other member. He can insist upon the Cabinet deciding in any matter in accordance with his own particular views; otherwise, he has the power of dissolving the Ministry by his own resignation of office. Ordinary questions, however, are generally decided by vote, the opinion of the majority, even though adverse to that of the Premier, being adopted. If any member desires a rearrangement of ministerial offices, he must make known his views to the Prime Minister. It is only the First Minister who can make changes in an Administration, subject, of course, to the approbation of the Queen. If he should vacate office, the Ministry is dissolved.

I have placed the Lord Chancellor second, instead of first, on my list of Cabinet ministers, because, though, in point of precedence, the Lord Chancellor is, with the exception of the Archbishop of Canterbury, the highest officer in the realm, yet the Prime Minister is regarded as the head of the Cabinet. The Lord Chancellor is a Privy Councillor by his office; a Cabinet Minister; and, according to Lord Chancellor Ellesmere, prolocutor of the House of Lords by prescription. To him belongs the appointment of all the justices of the peace throughout the kingdom. Being in former times commonly an ecclesiastic (for none else were then capable of an office so conversant with writing), and presiding over the royal chapel, he became keeper of the Sovereign's conscience; visitor, in right of the Crown, of all hospitals and colleges of the King's foundation; and patron of all the King's livings under the value of £20 per annum in the King's books. He is the general guardian of all infants, idiots, and lunatics; and has the general superintendence of all charitable uses in the kingdom. And all this over and above the extensive jurisdiction which he exercises in his judicial capacity in the Court of Chancery. In former times the Lord Chancellor was frequently Prime Minister. The Earl of Clarendon, in the reign of Charles II., was the last who occupied this position; but his successors in office have invariably been leading members of the Cabinet, and for this reason objections have often been urged against the union of judicial and political functions in the office of Lord Chancellor. But the advantage to the Cabinet in having the assistance of the highest equity judge is very great, whilst no injury has ever yet occurred to the interests of justice from the frequent changes of this functionary, which are incidental to parliamentary government.

The Lord President of the Council is an officer of great dignity and importance, though he no longer possesses the powers he anciently exercised. He presides over the department of the Privy Council, and has the patronage of its entire establishment. He sits next the Sovereign at the Council-table, to propose the business to be transacted, and to take her Majesty's pleasure thereupon. He has the general superintendence and control of the Education department (which I hope will soon have a special minister of its own), and has to frame minutes of Council upon subjects which do not belong to any other department of State. He is also responsible for appointing and summoning such special committees of Council as may be required from time to time, and for receiving their reports. Subordinate to his department are separate establishments in relation to public health, the cattle plague, and quarantine. The Lord President is generally a member of the House of Lords.

The office of Lord Privy Seal is one of great trust, though its duties are not very onerous, for they simply consist in applying the Privy Seal once or twice a-week to a number of patents. Ever since Henry VIII. the Privy Seal has been the warrant of the legality of grants from the Crown, and the authority of the Lord Chancellor for affixing the Great Seal.* All grants of the Crown for appointments to office, creations of honours,

---

* There are some important instruments, however, which pass under the Great Seal without warrants of Privy Seal—viz., patents of appointments of various Common-Law Judges and officers, and commissions for opening and proroguing Parliament, and for giving the royal assent to bills in Parliament.

patents of inventions, &c., must be made by charters or letters-patent under the Great Seal; and the command of the Lord Chancellor to prepare such a document is by means of a writ or a bill sealed with the Privy Seal, because the Queen cannot herself make letters-patent except by means of her ministers, who act according to her legal commands. The Lord Privy Seal is always in the Cabinet, and as his official duties are light, he is at liberty to afford assistance to the Administration in other ways, and he often has to attend to matters which require the investigation of a member of the Government. With regard to this official, a daily paper remarks:—"He is, as a rule, a man who has served the State in other capacities, and is conversant with the duties of probably more than one department. Released from official routine, he is in the first place free to assist his leader of the Upper House in debate, and to master any subject likely to come up for discussion. But beyond this obvious work there is a large part of statesmanship which consists in confidential investigation and preparative study. While the ordinary executive work of the country accrues from day to day, requiring daily decision and daily despatch, the work of renewing and reforming our legislation also demands the time and thoughts of our Cabinet. If every member of the Cabinet Council were, like the Secretaries of State, abundantly occupied with urgent affairs arising day by day, there would be nobody to forecast the necessary legislation, to note the currents of public opinion, to observe the signs of the times, to perceive the new needs that arise in the 'stress and storm' of modern competition and the daily struggles of our mixed society and affluent national life. The Prime Minister of the day has this duty imperatively imposed on him, but he requires *aides*. He cannot ask men cumbered with the reading and answering of a hundred daily letters or a score of serious despatches, and with the governance of hundreds of thousands or even millions of men, to turn aside from such pressing work in order to assist him in some preparative task intended to lay the basis of legislation, perhaps this session, perhaps next year. He wants for such purposes accomplished and experienced men, with the full sense of responsibility, and with ample leisure. No head-clerk, however able, could fulfil these conditions; and hence the use of retaining such offices as that of the Lord Privy Seal and the Chancellor of the Duchy of Lancaster, who may be in the Cabinet, but who have no heavy duties of their own, and can at any time be detached for temporary and special work."*

I now come to that important official, the Chancellor of the Exchequer. You know what a very thankless office his is, and how we hate the visits of his subordinates the tax-collectors. And not without reason — for if there be one people who fully and completely enjoy the privilege of being taxed,

* On July 26, 1870, Sir C. Dilke moved in the House of Commons, "that the sinecure office of Lord Privy Seal should be abolished." Mr Gladstone in reply said, "that some supply of great officers of State was really requisite for the discharge of public business over and above that which was furnished by heads of departments. It was scarcely possible to exaggerate the importance of the non-departmental business of the Cabinet. If men had their minds fully occupied with departmental subjects, it was not possible for them to give disengaged and concentrated attention to great matters wholly apart from departmental interests; but which, at the same time, it was absolutely necessary should be given by non-departmental members of the Government. Sometimes this arises in the case of bills which, though they may be brought to a particular department, were of such magnitude that they required the concentration of many minds. Take, for example, the bill relating to land tenure in Ireland. Though his right hon. friend the Chief Secretary possessed great ability and much knowledge of the subject, no department was equal to the formation of such a measure. He (Mr Gladstone) spent fully half his recess upon it, but neither he nor his right hon. friend could be alone equal to such a measure. The Cabinet bestowed a great deal of time on measures which it was absolutely necessary there should be men responsible for their introduction,

it is the inhabitants "of this bright little tight little island." The 'Edinburgh Review,' when describing our state of taxation many years ago, summed up our taxes in the following pithy manner: "Taxes upon every article which enters the mouth or covers the back or is placed upon

who should not be absorbed by other business. His noble friend (Lord Kimberley), who was Lord Privy Seal, but who had now got an office more worthy of his energies and abilities, was of the greatest assistance in the formation of the Land Bill. It was the constant practice of Cabinets to appoint committees, and upon these committees the most laboriously-worked heads of departments could not sit, as a rule. The Government were represented by six members in the House of Lords. Four of these—the Lord Chancellor, the Foreign Secretary, the Colonial Secretary, and the Indian Secretary—were hardly-worked officers of State; and with regard to the Lord President of the Council, he had to-day been asked whether, in consequence of the immense increase of duty which would be caused by the Education Bill, it would not be necessary to effect a separation of some of the duties of that department. The only adviser of the Crown in the House of Lords who, as a general rule, could take charge of measures not connected with particular departments was the Lord Privy Seal; and he could say that, for nine months of the year, the holder of that office was a fully-worked member of the Cabinet. There would be every desire on the part of the Government to give fair consideration to the subject, but they could not assent to the motion of his hon. friend."

The House divided—

For the motion,	60
Against,	170
Majority against,	110

the feet—taxes upon everything which it is pleasant to see, hear, feel, smell, or taste — taxes upon warmth, light, and locomotion—taxes on everything on earth and the waters under the earth—on everything that comes from abroad, or is grown at home—taxes on the raw material—taxes on every fresh value that is added to it by the industry of man—taxes on the sauce which pampers man's appetite and the drug that restores him to health—on the ermine which decorates the judge and the rope which hangs the criminal—on the poor man's salt and the rich man's spice—on the brass nails of the coffin and the ribbons of the bride—at bed or board, *couchant* or *levant,* we must pay;—the schoolboy whips his taxed top; the beardless youth manages his taxed horse with a taxed whip on a taxed road; and the dying Englishman, pouring his medicine, which has paid seven per cent, into a spoon that has paid fifteen per cent, flings himself back upon his chintz bed which has paid twenty-two per cent—makes his will on an eight-pound stamp, and expires in the arms of an apothecary who has paid a licence of an hundred pounds for the privilege of putting him to death. His whole property is then immediately taxed from two to ten per cent. Besides the probate, large fees are demanded for burying him in the chancel; his virtues are handed down to posterity on taxed marble; and he is then gathered to his fathers—to be taxed no more."

Many of these taxes are now happily obsolete, but still both you and I have often to thank that important functionary, the Chancellor of the Exchequer, for attentions we could readily dispense with.

The Chancellor of the Exchequer at present exercises all the powers which formerly devolved upon the Treasury Board. He has the entire control and management of all matters relating to the receipt and expenditure of public money, including even the private revenues of the Queen. He has to frame regulations, &c., for conducting the business of all the financial departments of the country, and also to control the expenditure and fix the salaries and expenses of every department in which there is an expenditure of public money. He decides within the limits of the law upon all questions between the Queen and the subject which may arise out of the receipt and expenditure of public money, &c. The annual estimates of the sums required to defray the expenditure of Government in every branch of the public service, though submitted to Parliament by the Cabinet collectively, are framed upon the especial responsibility of the Chancellor of the Exchequer. It is his duty to advise the House and the country in all financial matters, including the relations, the course, and the prospects both of revenue and expenditure. He lays before the House the annual statement of the estimated expenses of Government, and of the ways and means by which it is proposed to defray these charges, including the imposition or remission of taxes. This annual statement we call the "Budget," from the French *bougette*, a bag.

Since 1661 the office of Chancellor of the Exchequer has been combined with that of Under-Treasurer, which is properly the financial office, and by virtue of which he performs most of the functions anciently performed by the Lord High Treasurer. Formerly the Chancellor of the Exchequer was a principal officer of the Court of Exchequer and Receipt of Exchequer, but he has now very little to do with the former, and nothing with the latter. The only occasion on which he takes his seat amongst the Barons of the Exchequer is on the annual nomination of sheriffs. At the court which is held once in six years "for the trial of the pyx"—for determining the sufficiency in weight and fineness of the gold and silver coins issued from the Mint—the

Chancellor of the Exchequer, in the absence of the Lord Chancellor, has to preside and to deliver a charge to the pyx jury. When the office of Chancellor of the Exchequer is vacant, the seals of it are delivered to the Chief-Justice of the King's Bench for the time being, so that there may be no interruption in sealing writs, which issue daily from the Court of Exchequer. Thus, in 1757, Lord Mansfield continued nominally Finance Minister for three months; and, in 1834, Lord Chief-Justice Denman held the office for eight days. As a leading member of the Treasury Board, the Chancellor of the Exchequer has much influence in the disposal of the patronage belonging to it. I shall describe the duties of the Junior Lords of the Treasury and Joint Secretaries when I describe those officials of the Administration who are not Privy Councillors.

The Secretaries of State are the next most important officials[*] in a Ministry. The ancient English monarchs were always attended by a learned ecclesiastic, known at first as their *clerk*, and afterwards as secretary, who conducted the royal correspondence; but it was not till the end of the reign of

---

[*] They rank before the Chancellor of the Exchequer, but for convenience' sake I have included the duties of the Chancellor in my account of the Treasury.

Queen Elizabeth that these functionaries were called Secretaries of State. On the direction of public affairs passing from the Privy Council to the Cabinet after 1688, the Secretary of State began to assume those high duties which now render his office one of the most important in the Government. Up to the reign of Henry VIII. there was generally only one Secretary of State, but at the latter end of his reign a second Principal Secretary was appointed. In 1708 a third Secretary was created, owing to the increase of business consequent upon the Union of Scotland. But a vacancy occurring in this office in 1746, the third secretaryship was dispensed with till 1768, when it was again created to take charge of the increasing colonial business. In 1782 the office was again abolished, and the charge of the colonies transferred to the Home Secretary; but owing to the war with France in 1794, a third Secretary was once more appointed to take charge of the War Department, and in 1801 the colonial business was attached to his department. In 1854 a fourth Secretary of State for the exclusive charge of the War Department, and in 1858 a fifth secretaryship for India, were created, so that there are now five Principal Secretaries of State, four of whom, with their political under-secretaries, occupy seats in the House of Commons. One of the five Secretaries of State is always a member of the House of Lords. These Principal Secretaries have the sole control of the business of their respective offices—subject, of course, to the general superintendence of the Cabinet. They are the only authorised channels whereby the royal pleasure is signified to any part of the body politic, and the counter-signature of one of them is necessary to give validity to the sign-manual; so that while the personal immunity of the Sovereign is secured, a responsible adviser for every act is provided, who has to answer for what the Crown has done. Whatever be the number of the Secretaries of State, they constitute but *one office,* and are co-ordinate in rank and equal in authority. Each is competent in general to execute any part of the duties of the Secretary of State, the division of duties being a mere matter of arrangement. A Secretary of State is appointed directly by the Crown by letters-patent, and is removable at the royal pleasure. He receives his investiture by the delivery of the seals of office from the hand of the Queen in Council, and his appointment is formally terminated by the return of the seals to the Sovereign's hands. These seals are three in number—viz., the Signet, which contains the royal arms and supporters; another seal of a smaller size, having an escutcheon of the King's arms only; and a still smaller seal, called the Cachet, which is similarly engraved. The Cachet is only used for sealing the Queen's letters to sovereign princes. The Secretaries of State have to be in personal attendance upon the Sovereign on all public ceremonies and state occasions. During her Majesty's visits to various parts of the kingdom, a Secretary of State is always in attendance on her, and it is a rule that one must be always present in London. These high officers are always Privy Councillors, and invariably have a seat in the Cabinet; and as Cabinet Ministers, it is necessary that they should sit in one or other of the Houses of Parliament. Let me now briefly sketch their various duties.

The *Home* Secretary controls all matters relating to the internal affairs of Great Britain and Ireland. He maintains the internal peace of the United Kingdom, the security of the laws, and the general superintendence of the administration of criminal justice. He is responsible for the preservation of the public peace, and for the security of life and property throughout the kingdom. He is a magistrate, and can commit to prison by warrant for just cause. He exercises extensive powers over the civil and military authorities of the country, and has a direct controlling power over the administration of justice and police in the municipal boroughs, over the police in and around London, and over the county constabulary. He commits for trial, and examines persons charged with offences against the State, and delivers to their respective Governments certain fugitive offenders from France, the United States, or the Colonies. In connection with the Privy Council, he superintends the means taken for the local improvement and the preservation of the public health in towns. He has the general oversight and ultimate control of all matters relating to prisons, penitentiaries, reformatories, criminals, and the administration of criminal justice; and he is especially responsible for the exercise of the royal prerogative in the reprieve or pardon of convicted offenders, or the commutation of their sentences. The Home Secretary receives all addresses to the Queen (except those presented at levees), and all memorials and petitions, upon which he takes the royal pleasure, and acts as the official channel of communication between her Majesty and her subjects. He prepares all royal warrants, grants, patents, approbations of lords-lieutenant, &c., which do not belong to the departments of the other Secretaries of State or to the Treasury. The regulation of factory labour, and of labour in mines and factories, the inspection of fisheries and coal-mines, the supervision of pauper lunatics and lunatic asylums generally, the registration of births, marriages, and deaths, the registration of aliens, the granting of certificates of naturalisation, and various other duties, belong also to his department. The authority of the Home Secretary extends over England, Wales, Scotland, the Channel Islands, and the Isle of Man; and he is the organ of communication between the Cabinet and the viceregal Government of Ireland, for which he is personally responsible. Subordinate to him are the two law officers of the Crown, the President and Secretary of the Poor-Law Board, the Chief Secretary for Ireland, the Attorney-General for Ireland, and the Lord Advocate for Scotland. The Home Secretary, to assist him in his labours, has two under-secretaries, one permanent and the other political, and a staff of clerks.

The Secretary of State for *Foreign Affairs* is the official organ of the Crown in all communications between Great Britain and foreign powers. He negotiates all treaties and alliances with foreign states, protects British subjects residing abroad, and demands satisfaction for any injuries they may sustain at the hands of foreigners. He introduces to the Queen all foreign ministers accredited to the British Government; and it is his duty to inform the ministers of foreign Governments of any acts of his own Government or of her Majesty's subjects which may be liable to misconstruction, and to explain their nature and purport. For this reason he is in constant communication with the diplomatic agents of the British Government abroad, either by public despatches or by private diplomatic correspondence. No decision can be given in the Foreign Office to any business without his knowledge and consent—in fact, every paper of any importance whatever upon which any action is to be taken comes under the personal notice of the Foreign Secretary. All passports to native-born or naturalised British subjects going abroad are granted by this Secretary of State, and in his hands is the selection of all ambassadors, ministers, and consuls, accredited from Great Britain to foreign powers. The nature of the responsibility of the Foreign Secretary may be partly understood from the following extract from a letter of her Majesty read by Earl (then Lord John) Russell in the House of Commons, February 3, 1852. The Queen required, first, that the Foreign Secretary should "distinctly state what he proposes in a given case, that the Queen may as distinctly know to what she is giving her royal sanction; secondly, that having once given her sanction to a measure, it be not altered or modified by the minister. . . . She expects to be kept informed of what passes between him and foreign ministers before important decisions are taken based upon that intercourse, and to receive foreign despatches in good time, and to have the drafts for her approval sent to her in sufficient time to make herself acquainted with their contents before they must be sent off." Formerly the language in which diplomatic intercourse was conducted by the representatives of the British Government with the agents of foreign states was French, but now English is invariably employed, it being considered unbefitting the greatness of England to be dependent upon France for the language of diplomatic communications. No important political instruction is ever sent to any British minister abroad without its draft being first submitted to the Prime Minister, in order that the royal pleasure may be taken thereupon. "The leading features of our foreign policy are, to extend our commercial relations, not to interfere unnecessarily in the affairs of other countries, and to endeavour legitimately to promote the good government and prosperity of other countries." The Secretary of State is assisted in his labours by the political and permanent under-secretaries, an assistant under-secretary, and a staff of clerks.

In 1660 the direction of the colonies of England was intrusted to a committee of the Privy Council called the " Council of Foreign Plantations," which was afterwards consolidated with the Council of Trade, and was known as the " Board of Trade and Plantations." On the loss of a large portion of the North American colonies, the Plantation Board was abolished, and the remaining colonies placed under the charge of the Home Secretary. From 1801 to 1854 the business of the colonies was consolidated with the War Office; but in 1854 the two departments became separate, and each under the control of its own Secretary of State. The Secretary of State for the colonies has to superintend the government of the various colonial possessions of the British Crown. He appoints the governors over the different dependencies of the Crown, and sanctions or disallows the enactments of the colonial legislatures. He corresponds with the colonial governors, and makes such recommendations or suggestions as may be expedient to assist the deliberations of the colonial councils, and to promote the welfare of colonial subjects. In his hands is placed the responsibility of devising and submitting to Parliament laws peculiarly affecting the colonies, and in these matters he is often assisted by the Privy Council Committee for Trade. The Secretary of State for the colonies is directly responsible for every act of the governor of any of the colonial dependencies of the British Crown; and all colonial governors act under his immediate directions and instructions. All colonial enactments are brought under the consideration of this important officer of state, by whom they are referred to legal officers whose duty it is to examine and report upon every act, for the purpose of discovering any defect, and of determining the expediency of allowing or disallowing the same. Under the supervision of the Colonial Secretary is the Colonial Land and Emigration Board, which considers all questions relating to colonial lands, and the conveyance of emigrants to the various colonies. Owing to the establishment of responsible government in many of our colonies, the correspondence of the Colonial Office has much decreased; and as much of this correspondence is of a routine description, it is not necessary that every particular despatch need be submitted to her Majesty. The Colonial Office is divided into several branches, each of which takes cognisance of the affairs of a group of colonies. The despatches from the several colonies are examined in these departments, and ultimately by the Colonial Secretary, who is solely responsible for the replies sent to them. The Colonial Secretary is assisted by two under-secretaries—one political and the other permanent—and a staff of clerks.

Until the commencement of the present century, the control of the army was more in the hands of the Crown than in the hands of its responsible advisers. Before 1854 the direction of military affairs, although formally centred in the administration of the time being, was practically divided between the Commander-in-chief at the Horse Guards, the Master-General and the Board of Ordnance, the Secretary-at-War, and the Secretary of State for War and the Colonies. On the declaration of war against Russia in 1854, the duties of War Minister were, as I have just said, separated from those of Colonial Secretary, and a Secretary of State for War appointed, in whose hands the supreme and responsible authority over the whole military business of the country, formerly transacted by the various departments, was placed. In the following year, the separate departments of the Ordnance and the Commissariat, together with the office of Secretary at War and the control of the militia, yeomanry, and volunteers, were consolidated, and committed to the charge of the new War Secretary. The two great functionaries who now superintend the control of military matters are the Secretary of State for War and the Commander-in-Chief. The duties of the Commander-in-Chief embrace the discipline and patronage of the army, and the direct superintendence of the *personnel* of the army. His duties are carried on to a very great extent under the control and in every respect under the responsibility of the War Secretary. If irreconcilable differences should occur between the Secretary of State and the Commander-in-Chief on any question, appeal must be made to the Prime Minister or to the Cabinet, and the Commander-in-Chief must ultimately defer to their decision or retire from office. With the exception of the duties performed by the Commander-in-Chief, everything connected with the management of the army, in peace or war (its *matériel* and civil administration, &c.), remains in the hands of the Minister for War. During active service the War Minister has entire control over the operations as bearing upon the conduct of the Commander-in-chief, of the Admiralty, Transport Board, Commissariat, and even of the Treasury itself. It is his duty to combine the various powers of these departments in such a manner as to conduce to the proper management of the military operations of the country. As long as war continues, the operations of the War Office and the Admiralty, and the directions of the movements both of the army and navy, become a part of the special duty of the Secretary for War; but in time of peace the Admiralty is a totally independent office. When troops are required to be sent abroad, the matter is considered first by the whole Cabinet, and their decision communicated by the War Minister to the Commander-in-Chief, with instructions to take her Majesty's pleasure as to the regiments to be selected for the service. All general and other superior officers recommended by the Commander-in-Chief for commands or appointments must be first submitted to the Secretary for War (first commissions in the cavalry and infantry are, however, the peculiar patronage of the Commander-in-Chief). Should anything in the conduct of the Commander-in-Chief require the interference of the War Minister, not only has he the right but it is his bounden duty to interfere. As, however, the administration of the discipline of the army is intrusted to the Commander-in-Chief, the War Minister ought not to interfere, except under peculiar circumstances. To sum up the relations that exist between the War Secretary and the Commander-in-Chief, we may assert that the Secretary of State for War has the supreme authority and responsibility in all matters affecting the administration of the army; that he may act either directly himself or through the Commander-in-Chief, who is his military adviser, and subordinate to him; and that there is *no act* of the Commander-in-Chief that does not constitutionally come within the revision of the War Secretary, and for which he is not responsible. During a war the commanding officer reports direct to the Secretary of State for War, as the official organ of the Queen's Government, and receives his instructions. It is only upon strictly military details that he corresponds with the Commander-in-Chief. The Secretary for War, though he presides over the administration of the army unaided, has around him experienced professional advisers, whose opinions he often consults. His department consists of the Principal Secretary of

State, a parliamentary under-secretary, a permanent under-secretary with an assistant, a controller-in-chief—who has under him the barrack, commissariat, purveying store, and transport departments—an assistant controller, a military assistant, and numerous other officials. The Commander-in-Chief is not a Cabinet Minister; and as he is the executive head of the army, he exercises no *political functions*. His subordinate officers—the Quartermaster-General, Adjutant-General, and Military Secretary—are not allowed to have seats in the House of Commons.*

* Since these lectures were written, an Order in Council, defining the duties of the Field-Marshal Commanding the Forces, has been approved of by her Majesty. It states that, "subject to the approval of the Secretary of State for War, and to his responsibility for the administration of the Royal authority and prerogative in respect of the army," the Commander-in-Chief shall, in addition to the military command, be charged with the discipline and distribution of the army, and of the reserve forces when embodied or called out for actual military service; with the military education and training of both officers and men of the same; with enlisting men for, and discharging men from, the army and army reserves; with the collection and record of strategical information, including topography, in relation to the military circumstances of this and other countries; "with the selection of fit and proper persons to be recommended to her Majesty for appointment to commissions in the army, for promotion, for staff and other military appointments, and for military honours and rewards;" and with the duty of rendering such advice and assistance on

From the year 1784 to 1858, the territories belonging to the British Crown in the East Indies were governed by a department of State called the Board of Control, in conjunction with the Court of Directors of the East India Company. In 1858, however, this double government was abolished, and the entire administration of the British Empire in India was assumed by her Majesty, and all the powers formerly exercised by the East India Company and the Board of Control were transferred to

military affairs as may be required of him by the Secretary of State for War.

This Order in Council, however, asserts no new doctrine, but only affirms the old-established principle in thus making the actions of the Commander-in-Chief subject to the approval of the Secretary of State for War. To those acquainted with the question, there has never existed any doubt upon this point. The error has arisen from forgetfulness of the fact that the War Minister is the Minister of the Crown and not of Parliament; and that although he is responsible to Parliament for the advice which he may give to her Majesty, yet it is in the execution of the Royal authority and prerogative that he is superior to the officer Commanding in Chief. "The principle of our constitutional army is, that command, preferment, and honour come to it from the Crown ; but the general principle is equally undisputed, that for all pecuniary remuneration it is made to depend on Parliament." But by the Constitution the Crown exercises its authority only through responsible Ministers, and thus it follows that the Secretary of State for War is supreme over any other authority in the army, including the officer Commanding in Chief.

a fifth Principal Secretary of State. To assist this Principal Secretary in the transaction of Indian business, a Council of State for India, consisting of fifteen members, has been established, which meets at least once a-week, and is presided over by the Secretary of State, or by his vice-president. Questions are determined in Council by a majority of voices, but the Indian Secretary is at liberty to overrule the decisions of his Council on all questions but those relating to the appointment to the Supreme Council of India, or to the Council of the several Presidencies, and to the appropriation of any part of the Indian revenues: these questions must be decided by a majority of the Council. The Council is divided into six committees of five members each, every member being on two committees—viz., the Revenue, Judicial, Public Works, Political, Military, and Miscellaneous committees. Each committee is charged with its own particular branch of administration, and has to discuss all matters referred to it by the whole Council, or by the Secretary of State. In fact, the Council of State for India is the deputy of the House of Commons, exercising an efficient vigilance over the acts of the Secretary of State, and is to some extent a check upon the exercise of his otherwise arbitrary administrative powers, for there is no representative system in India to control his acts. The Secretary for India is, however, responsible for everything connected with Indian government at home and abroad, and must be prepared to defend in Parliament his conduct and policy. The whole of the Indian revenues are at the disposal of the Secretary and his Council, and they can draw upon these revenues for all expenditure required for the service of India, whether at home or abroad. An annual statement upon the revenue and expenditure, and upon the moral and material progress and condition of the country, known as the Indian budget, is presented to the House of Commons by the Secretary of State, and gives rise to a debate upon the policy of the Government in relation to India. The Governor-General of India, to whom the internal government of India is intrusted, and who is possessed of immense executive powers, is entirely subject to the constitutional control of the Sovereign, through this Secretary of State. Any law or regulation of the Governor-General or his Council may be disallowed by the Crown, upon the advice of the Secretary of State for India. The permanent establishment of the Secretary of State for India in Council consists of two under-secretaries, an assistant-secretary, and the Council already mentioned. The Secretary for India and one undersecretary are allowed to sit in the House of Commons, but the members of the Council for India cannot possess that privilege.

The origin of the Admiralty may be dated from 1512, when Henry VIII. created an office for the transaction of naval affairs, and commissioners were appointed to report upon the state of the ships to the Lord High Admiral, to whom the government of the Navy was then intrusted, and whose office was one of such dignity that it was frequently conferred upon a member of the royal family, and occasionally retained by the King himself. The first Lord High Admiral was appointed in 1385, but it is only from 1405 that an uninterrupted series of these high functionaries can be traced. In 1636, this office was for the first time put into commission, the great officers of state being the commissioners. During the Commonwealth, naval affairs were managed by a Committee of Parliament. From the date of the Restoration to 1673, James Duke of York was appointed Lord High Admiral; from 1673 to 1685 the office was a second time put into commission, but on the accession of James II. he again declared himself to be Lord High Admiral. In 1690, on account of the abuses of power by the

Lords High Admiral in the reign of the Stuarts, an Act was passed constituting a commission of Admiralty composed of men experienced in maritime affairs, through whose hands all orders for the management of the fleet were to pass. Such is the origin of the present Board of Admiralty. In 1702 the Earl of Pembroke was appointed Lord High Admiral for four months, and to him succeeded for six years in that office Prince George of Denmark. In 1827 the Duke of Clarence was appointed Lord High Admiral for a very short period; and, with these exceptions only, the Board of Admiralty has endured as first constituted until the present time.

The commissioners consist of the First Lord and four Junior Lords, who are called the Lords of the Admiralty. They conduct the administration of the entire naval force of the empire both at home and abroad, command the royal marines, control the royal dockyards, and have an exclusive jurisdiction in respect to harbours and inlets throughout the United Kingdom. The First Lord is the only officer of the Board who is a Cabinet Minister, and from his position he exercises supreme power, and is responsible for the whole naval administration, his authority being only limited by the necessity of carrying the naval lords with him in his measures, so long as they remain in office. As it is essential that he should be a Minister of the Crown, it is of necessity generally given to a civilian, for few naval officers properly qualified for the office would be found in Parliament. The duties of the First Lord are very responsible and laborious. He has the general supervision of every department in the service, the determination of all political questions, and the settlement of all questions connected with naval expenditure and the preparation of the naval estimates. The patronage of the Admiralty lies principally in his hands; in fact, about 9000 naval and 2000 civil officers are dependent upon him for promotion. In the exercise of this patronage, however, the First Lord can act only in conjunction with the Board. The commissions of all naval officers are from the Lords of the Admiralty, but commissions of officers of the marines are signed by a Secretary of State. As the Admiralty is but an executive Board, it is subject on certain matters to the control of the Government. The number of men required for the naval service is considered by the Cabinet, and the result of their deliberations communicated to the Admiralty, upon whom it devolves to carry out the decision of the Government. Again, the manner in which her Majesty's ships are to be distributed upon home or foreign service is a Cabinet question; and with respect to the strength of foreign squadrons, the Admiralty is guided by the Colonial and Foreign Offices. Any Secretary of State conveying to the Admiralty the Queen's pleasure must be implicitly obeyed by that department, for the Admiralty is subordinate to the Secretaries of State when they convey the royal commands. The duties of the Junior Lords I shall describe in the concluding portion of this lecture.

The President of the Board of Trade is always an important member of an Administration, as you will soon see when you hear what are the duties he has to perform. In 1660 Charles II. established two councils, one for trade and another for plantations, which were afterwards united as a board, and called the Board of Trade. In 1782 the Board was abolished, and affairs of trade were placed under the direction of a committee of the Privy Council. At the commencement of every reign this committee is appointed by Order in Council, and consists of a President, with certain *ex-officio* members—viz., the Archbishop of Canterbury, Lord Chancellor, First Lord of the Treasury, Principal Secretaries of State, Chancellor of the Exchequer, and certain Cabinet Ministers, with other Privy Councillors who do not form part of the Administration, but are added to the board or committee on account of their official position or special knowledge. But owing to it being inconvenient for these high officers of state to attend the committee meetings, the office has by degrees become departmental, so that at the present time the Board of Trade means the President, who, with the aid of his secretaries and official staff, transacts all the business assigned to this department. Until 1864 it was not necessary for the President to have a seat in the Cabinet; but since that time he has always been a Cabinet Minister, in order to insure for his advice on commercial matters a due consideration. It is his duty to take cognisance of all matters relating to trade and commerce, and to protect the mercantile interests of the United Kingdom; to advise the Foreign Office in commercial matters arising out of treaties or negotiations with foreign powers; the Home Office with respect to the grant and provisions of charters or letters-patent from the Crown; the Colonial Office upon questions affecting commercial relations with the colonies; and the Treasury as to contemplated alterations in the customs and excise laws. He has also to superintend the progress of bills and questions before Parliament relating to commerce; to exercise a

CONTROL OF THE BOARD OF TRADE. 109

supervision over railway, patent, telegraph, harbour, and shipping bills; to collect and publish statistical information; and to exercise a surveillance over all railway companies. United to his department are the Government School of Design, the offices for the Registration of Designs and Joint-Stock Companies, the General Register Office for Merchant Seamen, the Inspectorships of Lime and Alkali Works, of Oyster Fisheries and of Corn Returns, and the Standard Weights and Measures department. The Board of Trade also represents the general lighthouse' service in Parliament, superintends duties in connection with harbours and navigation under local Acts, and discharges duties under the Metropolitan Waterworks Act and the Fisheries Convention Act, together with various other duties, too numerous to mention to you here. To carry on effectively the work assigned to it, the Board of Trade is divided into six departments—the Commercial and Miscellaneous; the Railways and Telegraphs; the Mercantile, Marine, and Wreck; the Statistical, the Financial, and the department relating to Harbours, including Fisheries and Foreshores. Until 1867 there was a Vice-President of the Board of Trade, who was a Privy Councillor and a member of the Administration, though not a Cabinet Minister. He usually held his office in connection with that of the Paymaster-General, but now no such office as this exists, and the Board of Trade consists of only the President, two secretaries,—one of whom sits in Parliament,—four assistant-secretaries, and a large staff of clerks.

In addition to the First Lord of the Treasury, the Lord Chancellor, the Lord President of the Council, the Lord Privy Seal, the Chancellor of the Exchequer, the five Principal Secretaries of State, the First Lord of the Admiralty, and the President of the Board of Trade, all of whom are, *ex-officio*, Cabinet Ministers, there are some other members of the Administration who usually, but not invariably, have seats in the Cabinet; and these are, the Chancellor of the Duchy of Lancaster, the First Commissioner of Works, the President of the Poor-Law Board, and the Postmaster-General. In the present Gladstone Ministry the Chief Secretary for Ireland is also a Cabinet Minister. The Chancellor of the Duchy of Lancaster was an office in ancient times of considerable importance, but it is now practically a sinecure, and is usually filled by a leading statesman, whose time is at the service of the Government for the consideration of such important questions as do not come immediately within the province of other departments. He exercises jurisdiction concerning all matters of equity relating to lands held of the Crown in right of the Duchy of Lancaster.

In 1832 the public works and buildings of Great Britain were for the first time placed under the control of a responsible Minister of the Crown, and were assigned to the charge of the Commissioners of Woods and Forests. In 1851, however, the department of Public Works was separated from the Woods and Forests, and erected into a Board, under the name of the Office of Her Majesty's Works and Public Buildings. The Board consists of a First Commissioner, and of the Principal Secretaries of State and the President of the Board of Trade as *ex-officio* members. The Board has the custody and supervision of the royal palaces and parks, and of all public buildings not specially assigned to the care of other departments; and also the administration of sums voted by Parliament for the maintenance and erection of all such works. Besides various other duties I need not trouble you with, the Office of Works is intrusted with the task of providing free walks and parks for the recreation of the public, as well as access to the national buildings and collections. This Board is subject to the

Treasury. It has been often urged in Parliament, and with very good reason, that the Chief Commissioner, being merely the principal surveyor of the State, and his office a department for carrying out such public works as have been sanctioned by Parliament, his appointment should be permanent—in other words, independent of all changes of ministry. The condition of the Board of Works is far from satisfactory, and the manner in which it performs its duties has given rise to numerous stories. One of them is, that a castor came off a clerk's chair in a Government office, and as the Board of Works has to provide the furniture of all the Government offices and other public buildings, it was immediately communicated with to repair the defect. After a hundred and fifty letters and forms had been written and filled up, a van and ten men were sent by the Board for the offending chair. It was kept three weeks, and the day after it was returned the castor came off again. Since 1823 the Chief Commissioner has frequently had a seat in the Cabinet.

Before 1847 the administration of poor relief in England and Wales was intrusted to commissioners acting under the control of the Home Secretary, but owing to the amount of labour which devolved upon the Home Office, the Poor-Law Commissioners were erected into a Board in 1847. This Board consists of a President, to be appointed by the Queen, and of four Cabinet Ministers, who are members *ex-officio*,—viz., the Lord President of the Council, the Lord Privy Seal, the Home Secretary, and the Chancellor of the Exchequer. In 1867 the Poor-Law Board, from being a temporary commission, subject to renewal from time to time by Acts of Parliament, was made permanent, with a considerable enlargement of its powers. The President of the Board is responsible for all that is done, and his duties are exceedingly onerous. "There is not," said Mr Villiers, when President of the Poor-Law Board, "a question which may arise upon anything which affects the moral, physical, or economical condition of the poor, that must not be examined and decided by him; and in order that he may give a decision, he must read all the papers that bear upon the subject. . . . Besides all this, additional permanent business has been thrown upon the office by the transfer, within the last two years, from the Privy Council to the Poor-Law Board, of the management of the education of the poor, so far as it depends upon State grants." The President of the Poor-Law Board has also to determine all matters of complaint against medical men, and other officers charged with misconduct or neglect of paupers. He is assisted in his labours by two secretaries, one of whom is entitled to sit in the House of Commons, and is a political appointment, two assistant-secretaries, and a staff of poor-law inspectors and clerks. The President of the Poor-Law Board was first admitted into the Cabinet in 1859, and the first time the office was represented in the Lords was in 1867. The Irish and Scotch Poor-Law Boards are represented in Parliament respectively by the Chief Secretary for Ireland and the Lord Advocate.

The Postmaster-General, who is usually, but not invariably, a Cabinet Minister, is the last Minister I shall have to say anything to you about. It is only since 1831, when the offices of Postmaster-General of Great Britain and of Ireland were consolidated, that the appointment has been considered a political office. Until the accession of George IV. it was held by two joint-commissioners, expressly disqualified from sitting in the House of Commons on account of the office having been created in 1711, subsequent to the statute of Queen Anne, which declared that all *new offices* should render their possessors ineligible for a seat in the Commons. In 1866, however, an Act was passed rendering the Postmaster-General eligible for the

House of Commons. When he is a member of the Lords it is the duty of the Secretary of the Treasury to represent the department in the Lower House. The Postmaster-General has to negotiate postal treaties with foreign powers, to determine questions connected with the establishment of increased postal facilities at home and in the colonies (subject to the approval of the Treasury in pecuniary matters, for, as a revenue department, the Post-Office is subordinate to the Treasury), and to distribute the patronage of his department, which is very great. He has to report annually to the Lords of the Treasury upon the condition of his department, and these reports are invariably laid before Parliament. In addition to his former duties, the Postmaster-General has now the management of the Electric Telegraph also within the United Kingdom of Great Britain and Ireland. To assist him in his labours the Postmaster-General has a secretary, two assistant-secretaries, and a large staff of clerks.

I now come to the *last* portion of my lecture—viz., those members who belong to the Administration, but are not Cabinet or Privy Councillors, and here I shall be very brief. These officials are, the *Junior Lords of the Treasury*, who are chosen one from each of the three kingdoms, and who have hardly any departmental duties whatever, but undertake the less important business that belongs to the Treasury—superannuating questions, examinations into breaches of the revenue laws, receiving deputations, &c.; the *two Joint-Secretaries to the Treasury*, one of whom is called the Parliamentary and the other the Financial Secretary, who assist in the transaction of the business of the Board, and in preparing its decisions upon all matters submitted to it; in fact, through their instrumentality the whole Treasury business (under the direction of the political chiefs) is conducted, for the Board has little more than a nominal existence; the *Paymaster-General*, who has to pay all voted services and other charges connected with the naval, military, and civil expenditure, according as credits are given, from time to time, upon the public monies in the Bank of England by the Comptroller-General of the Exchequer, pursuant to applications from the Treasury (it is proposed to amalgamate his office with that of the Judge-Advocate General); the *four Junior Lords of the Admiralty*, three of whom are Naval Lords, and who have to attend to the composition and discipline of the fleet, the appointments of officers, the courts-martial, the superintendence of the various departments the Admiralty is divided into, &c., &c., whilst the fourth Lord, who is called the Civil or Financial Lord, manages the naval finances, the engineering and architectural works, &c., and sits in the House of Commons; the *Parliamentary Secretary to the Admiralty*, who is the mouthpiece and organ of the department in the House of Commons if the First Lord should be in the House of Lords; the *Parliamentary Under-Secretaries of State* for the Home, Foreign, Colonial, War, and India Offices, who have the general supervision of all that is done in their respective departments, and who, if any of their chiefs should be members of the House or Lords, have to represent their department in the House of Commons; the *Parliamentary Secretaries* of the Board of Trade and Poor-Law Board; the *Law Officers of the Crown*, who are the Attorney-General, Solicitor-General, and the Queen's Advocate-General, and who constitute the advisers of the Crown in all cases of legal difficulty. The Attorney and Solicitor General advise the heads of the departments of state in matters relating to common or municipal law, and in regard to all prosecutions proposed to be instituted against public offenders. They conduct the prosecution or defence in all cases where proceedings are instituted for or against any public department or servant of the Crown, or in obedience to the orders of Parliament. In all proceedings at law or in equity which involve the security of the Crown or the proper discharge of the royal functions, the Attorney-General is the leading advocate. He is the representative of the sovereign in the courts, and has to prosecute all public offenders. The Solicitor-General shares the labours of his colleague, and, in the absence of the Attorney-General, is empowered to execute every authority of the Attorney-General, his powers being co-ordinate. The Queen's Advocate-General advises the Crown in questions relating to civil and international law, but his appointment is not now considered a political one. I have but one more important official to add to my number, and then my list is complete—*the Lord Advocate of Scotland.* At the union of England and Scotland in 1707 the Executive Government of Scotland consisted of a Lord High Chancellor, a Lord Justice-General, a Lord Justice-Clerk, a Lord Privy Seal, and a Lord Advocate; but, by degrees, the entire political functions of these offices devolved upon the Lord Advocate, and he is now intrusted with the particular care of the whole Executive Government of Scotland, subject to a general control exercised over all his acts by the Home Secretary. The Lord Advocate is the principal public prosecutor in Scotland. He is assisted by a Solicitor-General and four junior counsel, termed advocates-depute. He is understood to have the power of appearing as prosecutor in any court in Scotland where any person can be tried for an offence, or in any action where the Crown is interested; but it is not usual for him to act in the inferior courts, which have their respective public prosecutors, called procurators-fiscal, acting under his instructions. He does not, in prosecuting for offences, require the intervention of a grand jury, except in prosecutions for treason, which are conducted according to the English method. The Lord Advocate is virtually Secretary of State for Scotland, and is intrusted substantially with the conduct of Scotch business in the House of Commons. The Queen's *Lord High Commissioner* to the General Assembly of the Church of Scotland, who is the representative of her Majesty at the meetings of the General Assembly of the Established Church of Scotland in Edinburgh, is to a certain extent a political office, but it is not invariably changed with the Administration of the day.

And now, in conclusion, let me make a few remarks regarding the co-operation of the Ministry with the Houses of Parliament. I have told you that the Ministers to whom the executive functions of the Crown are intrusted must sit in Parliament; and according to the confidence that Parliament—especially the House of Commons—has in them, so long will they be in power. If Parliament declare that the Ministers have forfeited their confidence, a change, no matter how long the Ministers may try to hold out, must take place. You see, therefore, that we really are a self-governing country. The Queen appoints the Prime Minister, the Prime Minister appoints his colleagues, his colleagues appoint their political subalterns, and then they all together work the machinery of the State. But if Parliament—and by Parliament I mean more especially the House of Commons—does not believe in its engineers, it moves a vote of want of confidence; and if carried, the Ministry resigns. So that the ultimate verdict upon every exercise of political power must be sought for in the judgment of the House of Commons, and the House of Commons means the people. Plenty of opportunities are offered to members of Parliament to exercise their duty as jurymen upon the actions of the Government, for it is necessary that every department of the State should be adequately represented in Parliament, either by the political chief of the department or by some functionary connected with the same, or by some other officer of Government who is specially charged to be the Parliamentary representative of the department. Nor should this representation be confined merely to one chamber, but should always, when practicable, include both Houses. If the head of a department is in the House of Lords, and has a seat in the Cabinet, his department should be represented in the House of Commons by an under-secretary or other subordinate officer, as the case may be. The Prime Minister is responsible for the distribution of the chief offices of Government between the two Houses of Parliament, and this task is far from an easy one. But as the House of Commons is now such an influential portion of the Legislature, it is considered advisable that a larger proportion of Cabinet Ministers should have seats in that chamber. In the first Cabinet of George III. only one of its members was in the House of Commons, and thirteen in the Lords. In 1783 Mr Pitt was the sole Cabinet Minister in the Commons. In 1801 four Cabinet Ministers were in the Commons and five in the Lords. In 1804 Mr Pitt and Lord

Castlereagh were, out of a Cabinet of twelve, the only Ministers in the Commons. In the Grenville Ministry (" All the Talents "), of a Cabinet of eleven, seven were in the Lords and four in the Commons. In 1809, of Mr Percival's Cabinet, six were Peers and four were Commoners. In 1812, of Lord Liverpool's Cabinet, ten were Peers and only two Commoners. In 1814 the Commoners were increased to four, and the Peers decreased to nine. In 1818, out of a Cabinet of fourteen, six were Commoners; and in 1822, out of a Cabinet of fifteen, nine were Peers. Since the Reform Bill of 1832 the leading members of Government have been more equally apportioned between the two Houses. In 1864 Mr Disraeli gave it as his opinion that the heads of the two great departments of the public expenditure—the army and navy—a decided majority of the secretaries of state, and, on the whole, the great majority of administrative officers, should have seats in the House of Commons. He showed that the constitution has provided for the adequate representation of the Government in the House of Lords by allowing but four out of the five Secretaries of State to sit in the Commons, and by requiring the Lord Chancellor, the Lord President of the Council, and the Lord Privy Seal to be chosen from amongst the

Peers. And, as a general rule, these principles are now followed more or less in the distribution of offices. The Prime Minister may be selected from either House.

The Ministry, by modern constitutional practice, is responsible for recommending to Parliament whatever laws are required to advance the national welfare, or to promote the political or social progress of any class in the country, though formerly the Ministers were only responsible for the fulfilment of their executive obligations, and for obtaining the sanction of Parliament to such measures as they considered necessary to pass. In fact, all important public measures are expected to originate with the Ministry; and though many important public bills have been introduced by private members, yet they have never obtained the sanction of both Houses of Parliament without the consent and co-operation of the Ministry.

And now, Gentlemen, I shall conclude this lecture—already too long, I fear—by quoting the admirable remarks made by Rowlands, in his work on the English Constitution, respecting the advantages of Parliamentary government. He says, the value of this form of government in bringing the "monarchy into unison with the freedom demanded and obtained by the other institutions of the Government and by the people, cannot be too highly estimated. It has changed the vague, precarious, and irresponsible authority of the ancient monarchs for an executive council, nominated by the monarch from the Peers and representatives of the people, but acting under the direct influence of the House of Commons, and accountable there for all its proceedings. It has relieved the King from the burden, and from the moral as well as actual responsibility, of directing or conducting the State affairs; and whilst he retains his high position as chief of the State, and the power of impressing his views of government on his Ministers when in office, and of selecting new Ministers when a change is required, he is not involved in the fluctuating fortunes of the rival statesmen who from time to time become his servants as Ministers of the Crown. With respect to the people, it has opened the road to the highest offices of the State to the ambition of all who can raise themselves to distinction in the House of Commons; and thus it places political power of the highest order in the most eminent and distinguished of the people themselves."

LECTURE III.

THE HOUSE OF LORDS.

"Nobility is a graceful ornament to the civil order. It is the Corinthian capital of polished society. *Omnes boni nobilitati semper favemus*, was the saying of a wise and good man. It is, indeed, one sign of a liberal and benevolent mind, to incline to it with some sort of partial propensity. He feels no ennobling principle in his own heart who wishes to level all the artificial institutions which have been adopted for giving a body to opinion, and permanence to fugitive esteem. It is a sour, malignant, and envious disposition, without taste for the reality, or for any image or representation of virtue, that sees with joy the unmerited fall of what had long flourished in splendour and honour."—BURKE, *Reflections on the Revolution in France.*

GENTLEMEN,—The subject of my lecture to-night is the House of Lords—that patrician assembly the members of which constitute the most brilliant aristocracy in Christendom. And if I detain you here a little while you must excuse me, for if there is one thing an Englishman likes to talk about more than another, it is about a lord; and as I have to talk to you this evening about not one lord but the whole assembly of lords, it is very natural that such an engrossing topic should run away with me a little. I have no doubt you remember an anecdote, mentioned in Boswell's 'Life of Johnson,' of a Dr Oldfield who was always talking about the Duke of Marlborough. One day he came into a coffee-house and said that his grace had spoken in the House of Lords for half an hour. "And what did he say of you, doctor?" said a surgeon present. "Of *me?* why, nothing," replied the doctor, astonished. "Well then, sir," said the surgeon, "he was very ungrateful, for you could not have spoken a quarter of an hour without saying something of him." The race of Dr Oldfields is by no means extinct. We all of us know *our* Dr Oldfield, and we also know how long he will be before he mentions *his* duke. The truth is, that we Englishmen have a great respect for the Peerage, let us try to hide it ever so closely. Mr Thackeray, who was one of the keenest observers of character, said "that there was not a man in England who would not be proud to walk down Pall Mall arm-in-arm between two dukes." And if our novelists portray life and character as they really exist, we see in their pages how dearly Englishmen love a lord, and all that belongs to him. The divinity which Shakespeare says hedges round a king is surely extended to the Peerage also.

Some time ago I made the acquaintance of a distinguished American officer who had fought gallantly in that terrible war against the South, and when peace was restored had come over to England to study our manners and customs. He was a thorough American, full of ideas of equality, and wondered how Englishmen could tolerate such "slick fooleries" as the Peerage and all that kind of thing; but gradually his democratic notions considerably toned down, and he took as kindly to the society of the great as any man I ever met. One day, when I had accused him of becoming a stanch supporter of the aristocracy (for he was always talking about our "British lords," as he called them), he vindicated himself in the following words: "I must own my impressions *air* somewhat changed since my arrival in this country. The social influence of your Peerage is so strong with all of you that I reckon I'm pretty considerable infected likewise. No matter whether you *air* Tories or Rads, it's all the same, you're both bit by it. I don't believe the Britisher who says he don't care for your lords.

He may rail at 'em, but it's only the spite of jealousy. Ask him to dine with a duke, and then see what answer he'd give; guess there wouldn't be much need of pressing the invitation. And it can't be otherwise as long as your peers occupy the high social position that they do among you. A lord with you is everything. If a man is related to a lord, he lets me know the fact before I've spoken to him for ten minutes. When I call upon your lovely women, I find the cards of the aristocrats uppermost in their card-baskets. You can't do anything without a lord. You can't get up a society of any sort or natur' without shoving a lord in as its patron or president. You put him into city companies as a director; into hospitals, asylums, bazaars,—into everything. A lord in the chair at a public meeting always draws; and, in fact, as far as my experience goes, I don't know when a British lord don't draw. Such being the case, I suppose I've caught the lord-fever likewise, in order not to be singular. Wal, sir, look at America, where we are all preachin' equality (bar niggers), and abusin' this demoralised speck of land of yours because you don't do as we do; why, if you send us a British lord, the dandies of New York and Boston stare at him as if he were a god, and do all they can to imitate *his* dress and *his* manners; and as for our women, why I guess that they would sooner marry a real live English lord than any man in all the States, Districts, and Territories of North America." And, with certain reservations, I am inclined to believe a good deal of what my American friend said.

Now, as Conservatives we profess openly to have a respect for our aristocracy—a healthy, honest respect, such as no Englishman need be ashamed of. We look upon the distinction of rank and honours as necessary in every well-governed State, in order to reward those who have distinguished themselves, and deserve well of their country. We respect the House of Lords, not because it represents the great bulk of the landed property* of the kingdom, but on account of the high personal qualities for which, as a class, its members are eminently distinguished. We believe that for cultivation, refinement, and moral worth, the aristocracy of England is superior

---

* In point of wealth, however, the House of Lords exhibits a standard which cannot be equalled in any other country. Take the Dukes of Northumberland, Devonshire, Sutherland, and Buccleuch, the Marquesses of Westminster and Bute, the Earls of Derby, Lonsdale, Dudley, and Leicester, and Baron Overstone, and where (in the mere matter of wealth) will you find their equals collectively ?

to that of any other nation. And therefore we are proud of our peers, and hope that the House of Lords will long continue to hold its high place in the State, and long enjoy its ancient privileges. My object to-night is not, however, to look upon the Lords in a social point of view, but as a legislative assembly.

The Parliament of the United Kingdom of Great Britain and Ireland is composed of the Queen, the Lords Spiritual and Temporal, and the Commons. The origin of Parliament is one of those things which, as Lord Dundreary would say, no "fellow can understand"—at least, few subjects have afforded to antiquaries more cause for learned research and ingenious conjecture. Not to weary you, however, with their abstruse investigations, suffice it to say that, during the earlier reigns after the Conquest, the spiritual and temporal Lords were the only members of the legislative and judicial assemblies of the realm; and though the opinions of an inferior class of the community were occasionally asked, the Commons had no real participation in the business of these councils before the forty-ninth year of Henry III. Indeed, it was not until the fifteenth year of the reign of Edward II. that it was enacted that the legislative authority of the realm should be in the King, with the advice and consent of the Lords spiritual and temporal, and Commons, in Parliament assembled. This was the first attempt at settling a free constitutional government. Originally the three Estates of the realm sat together in one chamber, and various dates have been assigned for their separation into two distinct Houses,—nor is it a question I need trouble you with. The House of Lords is now solely composed of the Lords spiritual and temporal. In the earlier Parliaments, the number of the Lords spiritual was generally greater than that of the Lords temporal. In the reign of Henry III. a hundred and twenty Prelates and only twenty-three temporal Lords were summoned. In subsequent reigns the number varied considerably, but the temporal Lords rarely exceeded the spiritual Lords in number. At the time of the dissolution of monasteries by Henry VIII., the spiritual Lords were equal in number to the temporal nobility. The Lords spiritual are the Archbishops of Canterbury, York, and Dublin (the latter only till 1871), twenty-four bishops of the Church of England, and three Irish representative bishops (the latter, owing to the Irish Church Bill, will cease to sit after January 1, 1871). The Lords spiritual have always had a seat in the

House of Lords, but by what right is not agreed—some saying that it was by virtue of their ecclesiastical office, or by their tenures as barons. The Lords spiritual, not being ennobled in blood, are now regarded as Lords of Parliament only, and not Peers.

The Lords temporal are divided into Dukes, Marquesses, Earls, Viscounts, and Barons, whose titles are all hereditary. They are called Peers, because, although there is a distinction of dignity among them, they are equal in all public actions; as, for instance, in giving their votes in Parliament or at the trial of any nobleman. The title of Duke, though first in rank, is by no means the most ancient in this country. It was first conferred on Edward the Black Prince by Edward III., whom he created Duke of Cornwall. Marquesses were originally lords of the marches or borders, and derived their title from the offices held by them. The first who was created a Marquess as a title of honour was Robert de Vere, Earl of Oxford, in 1198. Earls were in existence before the Conquest by the title of *ealdormen*, and to their hands the administration of the shires was committed. After the Conquest they were called *counts*, and hence the shires intrusted to them were called counties; but in course of time the original title of Earl was revived. Viscounts' were created for the first time in the reign of Henry VI. The first Viscount was John Beaumont. The title of Baron is a very old one, and was in existence long before the Norman Conquest. Unlike the House of Commons, the number of the members of the House of Lords is not limited. In the reign of Henry VII., the temporal Peers who were summoned to Parliament were only 29; at the death of Queen Elizabeth this number was increased to 60. The Stuarts again raised the number to about 150, which William III. and Queen Anne further increased to 168. On the Union of Scotland in 1707, 16 representative Peers of Scotland were added to the House of Lords. The two first kings of the House of Hanover continued to make additions to the Peerage, so that in 1760 that body amounted to 174. In the reign of George III., the creation of peers was freely resorted to by successive Ministers as an expedient for increasing the influence of the Crown. On the Union of Ireland in 1800, 28 representative Peers of Ireland were admitted to the House of Lords, and 4 Lords spiritual, to sit by rotation of sessions, of whom an Archbishop of the Church in Ireland was always to be one. Since 1800 numerous additions have constantly been made to the Peerage.' George III. created 388 Peers; George IV., 59; William IV., 55; and our present gracious Queen, about 110; so that now in this year of 1870 (in addition to the 30 Lords spiritual) there are sitting in the House of Lords 4 Peers of the blood-royal, 20 Dukes, 20 Marquesses, 127 Earls, 31 Viscounts, and 239 Barons—making a total of 471 Lords spiritual and temporal.

Peers are created either by writ or by letters-patent, the latter being the more usual way, though the former is the more ancient. But the writ of summons to Parliament does not ennoble, unless the person summoned to Parliament actually takes his seat there. The method by letters-patent is therefore the more secure way of conferring nobility on a man and his heirs, because the title is not lost by his omission to sit in Parliament. A writ of summons is, however, generally used when the eldest son of a peer is called up to the House of Lords in his father's lifetime, because there is no fear of his children losing the nobility in case he never takes his seat, for they will succeed to their grandfather. According to the ancient law-writers, the sovereign can create either a man or a woman noble for life; but this proposition was disputed in the debate in the House of Lords on the letters-patent conferring a life peerage on Sir James Parke as Baron Wensleydale. It was argued that the Sovereign was not warranted by precedents in creating peers for life, and that, even if such prerogative ever existed, it had become obsolete, as it was certain that no life peerages had been created for several centuries. It was also contended that a power in the Crown to grant such peerages might be attended with dangerous consequences to the independence of the House of Lords, as the advisers of the Crown, being unrestrained by the fear of permanently increasing the number of peers, might on some occasions, in order to increase their political power, advise an exercise of that power. In consequence of the decision of the Lords, Lord Wensleydale was subsequently created an hereditary peer.

From the time of the Conquest to the present day, there has been no breach in the continuity of the English peerage. The Lords who now sit at Westminster are the historical representatives of the Lords who sat at Merton six hundred years ago; but among them there is not a single lineal male descendant of one of the earls and barons created by our Norman kings, or of one of the barons assembled at Runnymede, or of one of the peers who fought in 1415 under the banner of Henry V. at Agincourt. The historic names of Northumberland, Marlborough, Newcastle, Bath, Buckingham, Suffolk, Dudley, Salisbury, Essex, Beauchamp, Grey de Ruthyn, Grey de Wilton, &c., are all borne by personages who at the best are heirs through females, and for the most part are connected by neither blood nor alliance with the ancient houses whose titles they have assumed.* Of existing dukedoms, only those of Norfolk and Somerset date before the reign of Charles II. Of existing marquessates only those of Winchester and Worcester were created before the reign of George III. Of the earldoms created by the Plantagenets and Tudors, eleven alone are still extant,—six of them merged in higher titles, the remaining five being

* The Dukes of Northumberland are not Percies, but Smithsons; the Wellesleys are not Wellesleys, but Colleys; the Pagets are not Pagets, but Bailys; Earl Nelson is a Bolton, not a Nelson; Lord Carington is not a Carington, but Smith; Lord Braybrooke and Lord Abergavenny, though owning the names of Neville and Nevill, have no blood of the Nevilles, Earls of Westmoreland, in their veins; the Earl of Warwick is no descendant of the Kingmaker; the Earl of Leicester is neither Plantagenet, nor Dudley, nor Sydney, nor even a Coke, but a Roberts; and Lord De Ros is not a De Ros, but a Fitzgerald. "Out of the twenty-five barons," says Sir B. Burke, "who were chosen to enforce the observances of Magna Carta, not one is at this day represented in the House of Peers by a genuine male descendant."

Shrewsbury, Derby, Huntingdon, Pembroke, and Devon. Of the sixty English peerages in existence at the death of Elizabeth, forty are now extinct.

Among the peers of Scotland and Ireland there are not a few who are the lineal descendants and heirs-male of the original grantees of their peerages. In Scotland there are Argyll, Athole, Montrose, Huntly, Angus, Abercorn, Perth, Caithness, Strathmore, Dundonald, Borthwick, Forbes, &c.; and in Ireland there are Kildare, Ormonde, Cork, Meath, Clanricarde, Kerry, Granard, Westmeath, Kinsale, Dunboyne, Fingall, &c.

Mr Disraeli has remarked in 'Coningsby' that our nobility owe their elevation to three principal causes: "The spoliation of the Church under Henry VIII., the open and flagrant sale of honours by the elder Stuarts, and the borough-mongering of modern times." But success at the Bar and behind the counter has always proved one of the most sure and certain means of attaining to a coronet. Lord Stanhope truly says that "it is this constant affluence which keeps the stream of the Peerage clear, and prevents it from becoming a stagnant and fetid pool. What has kept it firm and unshaken, while so many neighbouring aristocracies have tottered to decay or fallen before political convulsions? It is because their families are constantly coming from the people and returning to the people. They have been an institution, not a caste asserting for themselves and their descendants an inborn superiority over their brother men. With us, how many sons of ploughmen or weavers ennobled for their services sit side by side with the loftiest of the Somersets and the Howards!"

The founders of the families of the present Earls of Essex and Craven were William Capel, a draper, and William Craven, a tailor. The modern Dukes of Northumberland derive their male descent from Hugh Smithson, an apothecary, and the modern Earls of Warwick from William Greville, a woolstapler. The Earls of Dartmouth, Radnor, Ducie, Pomfret, Tankerville, and Coventry, are descended from a skinner, a silk-worker, a tailor, a Calais merchant, and the two latter from mercers. The ancestors of the Earls of Dudley and Romney were jewellers and goldsmiths, and those of the Duke of Leeds, the Earls Cowper, Fitzwilliam, and Darnley, Lords Dormer, Leigh, Hill, Dacre, Willoughby d'Eresby, and Carington, were all tradesmen of one kind or another. Lord Tenterden was the grandson of a barber, Lord St Leonards is the son of one; Lord Eldon was the son of a coal-agent, Lord

Clyde the son of a journeyman cabinetmaker, Lord Annaly of a money-lender, and Lord Carnworth and the first Lord Ellenborough of country clergymen. Lord Ashburton, Lord Overstone, Lord Belper, and Lord Wolverton, are instances in our own day of merchants, manufacturers, and bankers who have been raised to the Peerage.

In my last lecture to you, I said that Parliament can be assembled only by the act of the Crown; and I have no doubt many of you have in former times joined the ranks of a curious populace, to see her Majesty drive down to Westminster in state to perform the ceremony of assembling Parliament. And a fine sight is the House of Lords on that occasion! Viewed merely as a pageant, the opening of Parliament is always sufficiently effective to insure its annual return being looked for with eager interest — and you know how disappointed we all are when her Majesty stays away from this national ceremony. At twelve o'clock the doors of the House are opened, and very shortly afterwards both sides of the galleries are filled with ladies in full evening-dress—though the labours of the toilet are concealed under shawls and cloaks till the arrival of the Queen. Then come in the peeresses in little groups of twos and threes, and, after much talking and bowing to their friends, are introduced into their places by the messengers. The peers, in their robes of state, saunter up the House to their seats, or chat with the peeresses—thus relieving with their scarlet robes the light colours of the ladies' dresses, and making both sides of the House look like two rich parterres. As the time for the Queen's arrival approaches, the Lord Chancellor and the various judges take their seat on the bench in front of the Woolsack, and form a most formidable row! In the seats reserved for the diplomatic corps are the various ambassadors and ministers, covered with orders, and in all kinds of uniforms. The Lord Chamberlain, the Usher of the Black Rod, Goldstick-in-waiting, and the Sergeant-at-arms, are in attendance, and all is ready for her Majesty's arrival. At two o'clock a messenger enters the House, and requests "my lords and ladies to uncover." And then all the ladies remove their shawls, and show how gorgeously they are "got up," and how they disapprove of the theory that beauty unadorned is adorned the most. A long pause of expectation ensues, and then—the doors are thrown open, and the heralds enter two by two, bowing stiffly in their handsome awkward tabards as they pass before the rich Gothic, but to all appearance uncomfortable-looking, throne. They are followed by the great officers of the household and by the peers bearing the Sword of State, the Cap of Maintenance, and the Crown; and then appears her gracious Majesty. And now all rise and stand till the Queen, having ascended the throne, commands the House to be seated.

All being assembled, her Majesty desires the Lord Great Chamberlain, who commands the Gentleman Usher of the Black Rod, to let the Commons know that "it is her Majesty's pleasure they attend her immediately in this House." Up goes the Usher of the Black Rod to the door of the faithful Commons, which he strikes three times with his rod, and, on being admitted, advances up the middle of the House towards the table, makes three obeisances to the chair, and then says, "Mr Speaker, the Queen *commands* this honourable House to attend her Majesty immediately in the House of Peers." Like schoolboys let out for an extra holiday, away rush the Commons, with their Speaker at their head, to the bar of the House of Peers; and then her Majesty, in that clear silvery voice of hers, reads to both Houses of Parliament her speech, which is delivered into her hands by the Lord Chancellor kneeling upon one knee. The speech over, the House of Lords is adjourned, and the Commons retire from the bar. In the afternoon the House is resumed, and some bill is read a first time, as a matter of form, in order to show that Parliament has a right of deliberating without reference to the immediate causes of summons. This done, the Queen's speech is read by the Lord Chancellor, and afterwards by the clerk, and an address in answer to it is moved. Two members selected by the Administration now move and second the address, which is an answer paragraph by paragraph to the Queen's speech. The address, finally agreed to, is ordered to be presented to her Majesty. When the Queen does not open Parliament in person, the causes of summons are declared by the Lords Commissioners, and the programme of the ceremony is slightly changed. On such occasions the opening of Parliament is a mere matter of form and routine, and no spectacle whatever.*

Perhaps you have noticed, when paying a visit to the House of Lords in holiday time, a comfortable kind of ottoman in front of the throne. This

* During the last session (1870) Mr Gladstone introduced a Bill to amend the Acts of the 37th Geo. III., c. 127, and the 39th and 40th Geo. III., c. 14, by enabling the Government to assemble Parliament within six day, instead of fourteen days, after the public notification."

is the Woolsack, the seat of the Lord Chancellor. In the reign of Elizabeth an Act of Parliament was passed to prevent the exportation of wool, and to keep in mind this source of our national wealth, woolsacks were placed in the House of Lords, whereon the judges sat. The order in which the Lords are to sit is defined by an Act of Parliament, but it is seldom observed with any strictness. The bishops always sit together in the upper part of the House, on the right hand of the throne; the members of the Administration on the front bench, on the right hand of the Woolsack, adjoining the bishops; and the peers who usually vote with them on the other benches on that side of the House. The peers in opposition are ranged on the opposite side of the House, whilst those who desire to maintain a political neutrality sit upon the cross benches placed between the table and the bar. Every member of Parliament is under a constitutional obligation to attend the service of the House to which he belongs. Formerly a member of the House of Lords could serve by proxy by virtue of a royal licence, authorising him to be personally absent if he appointed another Lord of Parliament as his proxy: this has now been done away with, and the personal service of every peer is required. On ordinary occasions, however, the attendance of peers is not enforced by any regulation; but when any urgent business requires their attendance, it has been usual to order the House to be called over, and this order has sometimes been enforced by fines and imprisonments upon absent Lords. The Lords usually meet for despatch of legislative business at five o'clock in the afternoon, but they very rarely sit either on Wednesday or Thursday. The quorum of the Upper House is but three—a number palpably inadequate for a numerous deliberative assembly; and the average attendance of peers is very incommensurate with the number of those whose privilege it is to take part in the proceedings of this august body. But in the fulfilment of their legislative functions, the Lords have long ceased to take the initiative in the introduction of great public measures. Bills which concern the improvement of the law, and certain private bills, appropriately commence with the House of Lords, but, as a general rule, the House of Commons is not disposed to receive very favourably bills which do not originate with themselves. The province of the Peers is chiefly to control and amend the projects of legislation which emanate from the Commons, and any one who remembers the conduct of the Lords on past occasions, when conflicts between the two Houses were far more frequent than at the present day, cannot but own that the House of Lords, sitting like a court of review upon measures originating in the Lower House, has discharged this duty with singular success, maintaining at the same time its independence, and vindicating its responsible position as a branch of the legislature. And here we must bear in mind, that though by modern constitutional usage the House of Lords is precluded from making direct use of the powers which it originally possessed as an independent and distinct branch of the legislature, it must not therefore be assumed that its authority is of little account. "Its ancient rights, though dormant, have never been disallowed; and if there were any necessity, the House of Lords would be freely competent to claim its former privileges, and to assume a more active share in the legislation of the country." At the present moment the most distinguishing characteristic of the Lords is their judicature. They have a judicature in the trial of peers, in claims of peerage, and offices of honour, under references from the Crown; in controverted elections of the sixteen representative peers of Scotland, and in all questions touching the election of Lords temporal of Ireland;

but, most important of all, the House of Lords is the Supreme Court of Judicature in the kingdom, the appeal tribunal in the last resort, but having no *original* jurisdiction over causes of justice. In cases of impeachments by the Commons, the Lords try and adjudicate the charge preferred. Formerly the House of Lords claimed an original jurisdiction in civil causes, and over crimes without impeachment by the Commons, but those claims are now abandoned. Appeals in ecclesiastical, maritime, or prize causes, and colonial appeals, both at law and in equity, are determined by the Privy Council. To assist the Lords in their deliberations, the judges of the Courts of Queen's Bench and Common Pleas, and such Barons of the Exchequer as are of the degree of the Coif, the Master of the Rolls, the Attorney and Solicitor Generals, and the Queen's Serjeants, are summoned at the beginning of every Parliament, by writs under the Great Seal, to be "personally present in Parliament with us and with others of our Council, to treat and give advice." In former times the judges, as assistants of the Lords, held a more important place than they now occupy, as they had a voice of suffrage as well as a voice of advice. Their attendance was formerly enforced on all occasions, but they are now summoned by a special order when their advice is required. They sit on the woolsacks, and are not to deliver any opinion unless requested.

The House of Lords enjoys various privileges necessary for the support of its authority, and for the proper exercise of the functions intrusted to it by the Constitution. These privileges depend upon the law and custom of Parliament, or have been defined by statute. Every peer, as one of the hereditary counsellors of the Crown, is individually privileged to have an audience of her Majesty. The House of Lords, as a branch of the High Court of Parliament, has its own peculiar law collected out of the rolls of Parliament and other records, and by precedents and continued experience; and hence any matter concerning it ought to be discussed and adjudged in its own chamber, and nowhere else. The Lords, however, cannot create to themselves new privileges not warranted by the known customs and laws of Parliament. The House has power to commit to prison any one guilty of breach of privilege, and as a Court of Record to fine; nor can the causes of commitment be inquired into by courts of law. Thus in 1779 one Flower was committed by the Lords for a libel on the Bishop of Landaff, and though the prisoner applied to the King's Bench to be admitted to bail, his application was in vain. Again, in 1675, when Lord Shaftsbury was committed by the Lords for contempt, the King's Bench stated that it had no jurisdiction over the cause. According to a standing order of the Lords, it is a breach of privilege to publish in print anything relating to the proceedings of the House without leave of the House. Thus, in 1801, Allan M'Leod was fined £100, and committed to Newgate, for publishing certain paragraphs, purporting to be a proceeding of the House, which had been ordered to be expunged from the Journal, and the debate thereupon; and in the same year two persons connected with the 'Morning Herald' were committed to the custody of the Black Rod for publishing an account of what passed in debate, but which the Lords declared to be a scandalous misrepresentation. However, notwithstanding the order of the Lords, so long as debates are faithfully reported in the newspapers, the privilege which prohibits their publication is waived. But when they are reported *malâ fide*, the publishers of newspapers are liable to censure. Libels upon the House of Lords have always been resented and punished as breaches of privilege, and fines, imprisonments, and in former times the pillory, have been adjudged for these offences. Prosecutions at law have also been ordered against the parties. Reflections upon members of the House of Lords are also severely punished as insults to the House itself. Without entering too much into details, we may say that disobedience to the rules of the House, indignities offered to the character or proceedings of the House, assaults upon its members, interference with the officers of the House in discharge of their duty, or tampering with witnesses about to give evidence, are the chief breaches of privilege. Should a peer, however, make a frivolous complaint of a breach of privilege, and the House adjudge that there is no ground for such complaint, satisfaction would be ordered by the House to the person complained of.

Another great privilege which the House of Lords possesses, in common with the Lower House, is the freedom of speech. By the Bill of Rights it is declared that "the freedom of speech and debates or proceedings in Parliament ought not to be impeached or questioned in any court or place out of Parliament." Should a peer, however, be guilty of using offensive words before the House, he can be called to account and punished by the House itself. Nowadays, members who make intemperate speeches generally satisfy the House with an explanation or apology. All published reports of debate are ignored by Parliament, and what is said in Parliament is supposed to be unknown elsewhere, and cannot be noticed without a breach of privilege.

Another privilege belonging to the Peers, and which is shared by the Commons, is freedom from arrest and molestation during the time of Parliament. This privilege is not claimable for any indictable offence—such as treason, felony, or breach of the peace. No action against a peer need, however, be stayed under pretence of privilege of Parliament, for he may be coerced by every legal process, except the attachment of his person. In cases of treason and felony a peer is tried by his brother peers, but in mere misdemeanours he is tried like a commoner by jury. A peer loses his nobility by attainder or by execution. Should he be condemned to death, as in the case of Earl Ferrers, he has the privilege (I don't know whether it is an advantage) of being hanged with a silken cord instead of a rope of vulgar hemp.*

Now, Gentlemen, I believe you very often have de-

* The rights of the Peerage have lately obtained recognition in one important point, for at length it has been finally established that a Peer of the Realm can be made a bankrupt like any ordi-

bates and discussions among yourselves in this room, so that an account of how a debate is conducted among the highest of the land may not be uninteresting to you, and perhaps give you a hint or two. When the Lord Chancellor takes his seat on the Woolsack, business commences. The Speaker of the Lords is generally the Lord Chancellor,* but

nary mortal. The fact is settled by the result of the appeal to the House of Lords in the case of the Duke of Newcastle. More than a hundred years ago, in a case then before Lord Chancellor Hardwicke, the eminent legist held that, "though there may be some particular powers which Commissioners of Bankrupts could not exercise against a Peer, yet, notwithstanding this, he may be liable to a commission of bankruptcy if he will trade; and so may a member of the House of Commons, though, while he continues a member, there are some particular powers of Commissioners that cannot be exercised against him." In all the Bankruptcy statutes since passed, there is nothing to weaken the authority of that dictum; and, by abolishing the distinction between traders and non-traders, the Act of 1861 rendered the Duke liable to that beneficial procedure which distributes the property of an insolvent debtor among his creditors. The only privilege which he can claim is exemption from arrest. It is important to the whole community that attendance on Parliament should be uninterrupted and absolutely free, and upon that ground alone members of the legislature are exempt from certain processes. But there is no constitutional reason for releasing them from making equitable arrangements with their creditors, or for excluding them from the provisions of our Bankruptcy Law.

* "It is a proud thing for the Commons of England to see one of their number, a private individual, elevated from obscurity

should the Chancellor be absent, the Lords may choose their own Speaker to supply his place. And it is a curious fact that the Lord Speaker of the Upper House is not necessarily a member. It has even happened that the Lord Keeper of the Great Seal has officiated for years as Speaker, without having been raised to the Peerage. When the Great Seal is in commission, the Chief Justice of the Court of Queen's Bench or Common Pleas, the Chief Baron of the Exchequer, or the Master of the Rolls, if a peer, is appointed Speaker. Unlike the Speaker of the House of Commons, the Speaker of the Lords is invested with no more authority than any other member, and (if a peer) has to address the House from his own place as a peer, and not from the Woolsack, for the Woolsack is not strictly within the House. The Chairman of the Lords' Committees is the Deputy Speaker.

At the table of the House is the clerk of the Parliaments, attended by the clerk-assistant and the reading-clerk, to take down minutes of all the proceedings.

solely by the force of talent and industry, taking precedence of the Howards, the Talbots, and the Percies—of the pride of Norman ancestry equally with the splendour of royal descent."—GEORGE CANNING.

ETIQUETTE RESPECTING SPEECHES. 153

The etiquette of the House directs that every peer as he enters is to give and receive salutations from the rest, and not to sit down till he has made an obeisance to the cloth of estate. During the debate he is to keep his place as much as possible, but when he is obliged to cross the House he is to bow to the cloth of estate, and on no account is he to pass in front of a peer who is addressing their Lordships. He is not to read books or papers for amusement, or for business unconnected with the debate. If he wishes to speak to a peer while the House is sitting, both have to go below the bar, and there converse. Whilst a peer is speaking, he must not be disturbed by hissing, exclamations, or other interruptions. As, however, the use of the Parliamentary expression "Hear, hear" is permitted, and as those words may mean approval, dissent, derision, or contempt, they often prove a very efficacious interruption. Peers, when they speak, address themselves "to the rest of the Lords in general," and not to the Speaker, as do the Commons.

No written speeches are permitted, but a member may refresh his memory by a reference to notes. Extracts from documents may be read, but the Speaker's own language must be delivered *bona fide*, in the form of an unwritten composition. When a peer addresses the House, he rises in his place and stands uncovered. Should he be sick or infirm, the indulgence of a seat is frequently allowed him. During a division, however, with closed doors, peers speak sitting and covered; but this practice is confined to questions of order arising out of the division, and does not apply to distinct motions proposed for the adoption of the House. The right of a peer to address their Lordships depends solely upon the will of the House. When two Lords, each supported by a party, rise at the same time, unless one immediately give way, there is no alternative but a division.* If the Lord Chancellor rises from the Woolsack to address the House, it is customary to give him precedence over other peers who may rise at the same time. A peer, when addressing the House, is only entitled to be heard upon the question then under discussion; and whenever he wanders from it, he is

---

* On June 13, 1870, Lord Stratheden moved a Standing Order, enabling the occupant of the Woolsack to decide which of candidate peers for a speech is to be heard, instead of the decision, as now, resting with the House in general. It was a good deal discussed, and met with some support; but, on the whole, their Lordships preferred to stand on their old ways, and the motion was withdrawn.

liable to be interrupted by cries of "Question!" These cries do not always signify that the speaker is being accused of irrelevancy, but that the House is not disposed to listen to him. Considerable laxity, however, prevails in allowing irrelevant speeches upon questions of adjournment. No peer may speak except when there is a question already before the House. Two exceptions to this rule exist —first, when putting questions to Ministers of the Crown, or to other members of the House, concerning any measure pending in Parliament or other public event; and, secondly, when explaining personal matters. In the Lords a greater licence of debate is permitted in putting and answering questions than in the Commons, without any question being before the House. A peer is not allowed to speak twice to the same question, except to explain some part of his speech which has been misunderstood, or, in certain cases, to reply at the end of a debate, or in commitee.

In order to preserve decency and regularity in debate, various rules have been laid down by both Houses of Parliament, which in the Lords are enforced by the House itself, and in the Commons by the Speaker; and as these rules are the same in both Houses of Parliament, I shall defer alluding to them, as well as entering into any explanations of the technicalities of Parliamentary language, till my lecture on the Commons. To guard against all appearance of personality in debate, no peer refers to another by name, but every Lord is alluded to by the rank he enjoys, as the "Noble Marquess" or the "Right Reverend Prelate," &c. Whenever any disorderly words are used by a peer in debate, notice should be immediately taken of them; and if any member desires that they be taken down, and the House agrees, the words are taken down *instanter* by the clerk, and the matter is dealt with as the House thinks fit.

Any Lord in the Upper House may submit a motion for the decision of their Lordships without it being seconded by another peer; and the sense of the House is not judged, as in the Commons, by "*Ayes*" and "*Noes,*" but by "*Contents*" and "*Non-contents.*"

Until 1857, a division was effected in the Lords by the non-contents remaining within the bar, and the contents going below the bar, but now the following plan is adopted: The lobbies on the right and left of the House are cleared of strangers, and the doors locked. The Lord Speaker appoints two tellers for each party; the *contents* then go into the right lobby, and the *non-contents* into the left, and on returning to the House are counted by the tellers, and their names recorded by the clerks. The votes being counted, they are announced to the Lord Speaker, and alphabetical lists of the names are printed with the votes. In case of an equality of voices the *non-contents* have it, and the question is declared to have been resolved in the negative. This rule is, however, altered when the House is sitting judicially; for if the numbers are equal, the House, on such an occasion, refuses to reverse the judgment of the court below. As a general rule, none but "law lords," or, in other words, peers who have held high judicial offices, vote in judicial cases, or otherwise interfere with the decisions of the House. All peers are, however, entitled to vote if they think fit. Thus in 1689, on the writ of error of that consummate scoundrel Titus Oates, the judgment of the court below was affirmed on a division by thirty-five peers against twenty-three, in opposition to the unanimous opinion of the nine judges who attended, and various other precedents have also confirmed their right, but it is now seldom enforced. In addition to the power of expressing assent or dissent by a vote, peers may record their opinions by a *protest*, which is entered in the Journals of the House of Lords, with the names of all the peers who concur in it. When important matters have to be deliberated upon, they are generally discussed in what is called a Committee of the whole House, presided over by a chairman instead of by the Lord Speaker. Such committees can, however, consider (except under certain special circumstances) only those matters which have been committed to them by the House. A peer in committee is allowed to speak more than once, so that the details of a bill or a question may have the most minute examination, and arguments may be used for and against. A *select* committee is composed of certain members appointed by the House to consider matters, and to report their opinions for the information of the House. Inquiry by means of evidence is the chief object of a select committee; but during the examination of witnesses, strangers are rarely allowed to be present, though in the Commons their presence is generally permitted. In examining witnesses the House of Lords has the power to administer an oath, and false evidence is liable to the penalties of perjury. The Commons cannot administer an oath to witnesses.

The Lords and Commons, as you may well imagine, have frequent occasion to communicate with each other respecting matters connected with the proceedings of Parliament. These communications are generally effected by a *message*, which is the simplest mode of communication, or by a *conference* composed of deputies from both Houses, which is more formal and ceremonious than a message, and is usually held in the " Painted Chamber," when the Lords sit covered, and the Commons stand and are uncovered. Joint and select committees of both Houses are also occasionally employed for this purpose.

Now I think I need hardly tell you that the chief duty of Parliament is to pass bills; but as regards this subject, I shall wait till I have to talk to you about the Commons. Bills may originate in either House, but the exclusive right of the Commons to grant supplies, and to impose and appropriate all charges upon the people, renders it necessary to introduce by far the greater proportion of bills in the House of Commons. All bills for the restitution of honours and in blood, however, commence with the Lords. Bills of Pains and Penalties, or, in other words, Acts of Parliament to attaint particular persons of treason and felony, or to inflict pains and penalties beyond or contrary to the common law to serve a special purpose, have also generally originated in the Upper House. Any peer is at liberty to present a bill, and to have it laid upon the table; but in the Commons a member must obtain permission from the House before he can do so. When a bill has passed the Lords it is sent down to the Commons by the clerk of the Parliaments for their concurrence. Should it be returned with amendments which are disagreed to by the Lords, a message is sent to the Commons, or a conference takes place for the purpose of discussing the reasons for such disagreement, and, if possible, by mutual concession to arrive at an ultimate agreement. If such agreement cannot be secured, the bill is lost for the session. When bills have been finally agreed to by both Houses, they only wait for the royal assent to give them the perfection of a law, and for this purpose they remain in the custody of the Clerk of the Enrolments in the House of Lords. With the exception of money bills, which are returned to the Commons, the Royal Assent may be given by the Sovereign in person, robed, crowned, and seated on the throne in the House of Lords, the Commons standing at the bar; or by Commissioners appointed by the Crown for that special purpose, and for the single occasion. The latter plan is now generally adopted, except when the Queen attends to prorogue the Parliament. The moment the royal assent has been given, that which was a bill becomes an Act, and instantly has the force and effect of law, unless some time for the commencement of its operation should have been specially appointed.

Queen Elizabeth, at the end of one session, rejected forty-eight bills agreed to by both Houses. The power of rejection was exercised in the year 1692 by William III., who at first refused, but two years afterwards yielded, assent to the bill for triennial parliaments; and for the last time in 1707, when Queen Anne refused her assent to a Scotch Militia Bill.

And here let me tell you that, with regard to Money Bills, the Lords have no power whatever to change or alter them; their functions are reduced to a simple assent or negative; and if they attempted to amend them, the Commons would at once remonstrate, and haul the Peers severely over the coals. As a co-ordinate branch of the legislature, the Lords can withhold their assent from any bill; and in former times their power of rejecting a Money Bill was expressly acknowledged by the Commons; but as for centuries they have forborne to exercise this power, it is now not admitted. In 1860, as you well know, the Lords refused their assent to the

Paper Duties Repeal Bill, and the matter was only settled by the Commons including the repeal of the Paper Duty in a general financial measure (and not as a separate bill) for the service of the year, which the Lords were constrained to accept. Since that time the budget of each year has been comprised in a general Act. The progress of local or private bills through the Lords is beyond the object of this Lecture.

I have one more thing to tell you with regard to the House of Lords, and then I shall conclude. I have no doubt that when reading your English history you have come across the word *impeachment*, and perhaps have not known its exact meaning. Impeachment is a prosecution by the House of Commons before the House of Lords of a commoner for treason or other high crimes and misdemeanours, or of a peer for any crime. It is a proceeding of great importance, involving the exercise of the highest judicial powers of Parliament; and though in modern times it has been rarely resorted to, in former days it was of frequent occurrence. The last cases of impeachment are those of Warren Hastings in 1788, and Lord Melville in 1805. No royal pardon can screen an offender from an impeachment by the

House of Commons. The mode of impeachment is this :—

A member of the House of Commons charges the accused of certain high crimes and misdemeanours, and moves that he be impeached: if the House agree to it, the member is ordered to go to the Lords, and at their bar, in the name of the House of Commons and of all the Commons of the United Kingdom, to impeach the accused. A committee is then appointed to draw up articles of impeachment, which are reported to the House, and having been discussed and agreed upon, are delivered to the Lords. After these preliminaries, the Lords appoint a day for the trial. The Commons desire the Lords to summon the witnesses required to prove their charges, and appoint managers to conduct the proceedings. Westminster Hall has been usually fitted up as the court, which is presided over by the Lord High Steward. The Commons attend with the managers, as a committee of the whole House. The accused remains in the custody of the Usher of the Black Rod, to whom he is delivered,—if a commoner, by the Serjeant-at-Arms attending the House of Commons. Persons impeached of treason are entitled to make their full defence by counsel; a privilege which is also enjoyed by persons charged by the Commons with high crimes and misdemeanours. When the managers have made their charges, and adduced evidence in support of them, the accused answers them, and the managers have a reply. The Lord High Steward then puts to each peer, beginning with the junior baron, the question upon the first article, whether the accused be guilty of the crimes charged therein. The peers, in succession, rise in their places when the question is put, and, standing uncovered, and laying their right hands upon their breast, answer "guilty" or "not guilty," as the case may be, "upon my honour." Each article is proceeded with separately in the same manner, the Lord High Steward giving his own opinion the last. The numbers are then cast up, and being ascertained, are declared by the Lord High Steward to the Lords, and the accused is acquainted with the result.

And here, Gentlemen, I shall conclude, though I have not told you all I might about my subject; for I remember the story of the lecturer on natural history, who, whilst exhausting the patience of his audience by the most minute accounts of almost every living creature under the sun, was interrupted by some one calling out to him that he had said nothing of the oyster. The naturalist thereupon began a very learned description of that mollusc, but his interrupter again stopped him very soon by saying that he had forgotten the one great advantage the oyster possessed over man. "And pray, sir, what is that?" said the lecturer. "Why, sir," replied the interrupter, "he knows when to *shut up!*" But, Gentlemen, in conclusion, let me make one or two remarks regarding the legislative utility of the House of Lords. You hear very often those who differ from us in politics assert that the House of Lords is next door to useless, and that it ought to be abolished. It ought *not* to be abolished. Sitting like a court of review upon measures originating in the Commons, the Lords have great facilities for estimating the direction and strength of public opinion. Nearly every measure has been fully discussed before they are called upon to consider it, and hence they are enabled to judge at leisure of its merits, its defects, and its popularity. If the people are indifferent to its merits, they can reject it altogether; if too popular in principle to be rejected, they may qualify it by amendments; and by their debates they are able to exercise an extensive influence upon the convictions of the people. Besides, history furnishes us with abundant proofs of the utility of the House of Lords in restraining the

Crown from exercising undue power, and the House of Commons from exceeding its constitutional authority. We all know how much we are indebted in the early stages of our history to the barons. It was to the barons that we owe that great bulwark of our liberties, Magna Carta, and its successive confirmations. It was to the co-operation of the Lords that we owe the Petition of Right, the independence of our judges, by the continuance of their offices being secured to them during their good behaviour, the abolition of the odious Star Chamber, and the maintenance of many privileges of Parliament in opposition to the wishes of the Crown. It was owing to the careful scrutiny of the House of Lords that the Commons in past days were prevented from acquiring unconstitutional power. It was the House of Lords that, in all cases of impeachment by the Commons, compelled the Lower House to proceed according to law, as is shown in the impeachments against the Earl of Clarendon in 1667, against the Lord Treasurer Danby in 1678, and against Lord Somers in 1701. It was the Lords who defended the rights of the people against a would-be arbitrary House of Commons in the reign of Queen Anne. Witness their resolutions in 1702 not to pass any money bill sent from the Commons to which any clause was tacked that was foreign to the bill; their address to the Queen in 1704, complaining of the conduct of the Commons in stopping the issue of writs; and again, their firm opposition to the Commons in the great cases of Ashby *v.* White and the Aylesbury men, in 1704-5. And in modern times, the conduct of the House of Lords on several important occasions, when the two Chambers have been at variance, proves that the existence of a House of Lords is a necessity in the State, to prevent encroachments of the executive or legistive government upon the rights of the subject. But what check, say you, is there against the encroachments of the Lords? Only one, but yet a most powerful one. It is this—the royal prerogative of creating new peerages; but a wholesale creation of peers for the purpose of obtaining a majority in the Upper House has been extremely rare.* Tak-

* As a general rule, when a Minister wishes to augment the number of votes in the Upper House without permanently increasing the British Peerage, he effects his purpose by advising that the eldest son of a peer be called up in his father's lifetime. This plan was frequently adopted during the last century, and several instances of its adoption occur also during the present century. Thus, the third Duke of Northumberland, in 1812, was called to the Upper House in his father's ancient barony of Percy; the late Marquess of Cholmondeley, in 1821, as Lord Newburgh; the late Marquess Camden, in 1834, as Baron Camden; the present

ing, therefore, all these things into consideration, I think, Gentlemen, we are right in not wishing for the abolition of the Lords; and notwithstanding the prophecies of our Radical friends, that "the House of Lords must go," we hope, on the contrary, that they will "go" first, and that the Upper House will long remain after their departure. As an additional argument in favour of a division in the legislature, remember this, that Oliver Cromwell constituted an Upper House to interpose "between him and the tumultuous and popular spirits in the Commons' House."

It is, however, greatly to be regretted that the Marquess of Ailesbury, in 1838, as Lord Bruce; the late Marquess of Anglesey, in 1832, as Lord Paget; the late Duke of Leeds, in 1838, as Lord Osborne; the thirteenth Duke of Norfolk, in 1841, as Lord Maltravers; the father of the present Earl of Stamford, in 1832, as Lord Grey of Groby; the present Earl of Tankerville, in 1859, as Lord Ossulston; the late Marquess of Lansdowne, in 1856, as Lord Wycombe; the late Earl Fortescue, in 1839, and the present Earl also, in 1859, as Baron Fortescue; the present Earl of Strafford, in 1853, as Baron Strafford; the eldest son of the present Duke of Somerset, Lord St Maur, in 1863, as Baron Seymour; the late Earl of Ashburnham, in 1864, as Baron Ashburnham; the late Duke of Bedford, in 1832, as Lord Howland; the late Earl of Gosford, in 1847, as Lord Acheson; the late Duke of Hamilton, in 1807, as Lord Dutton; the present Earl of Lonsdale, in 1841, as Baron Lowther; the fifth Duke of Marlborough, about the year 1807, as Lord Spencer; and the late Duke of Sutherland, in 1826, as Lord Gower.

House of Lords displays such passive indifference in the business of legislation, by an attendance (unless great party questions are under discussion) more befitting a select committee than an important branch of the legislature. Three peers may wield all the authority of the House, and it is hardly natural that the judgment of so small a number should be as much respected as that of the large bodies of members who throng the House of Commons. The Tenure and Improvement of Land (Ireland) Bill, which had occupied weeks of discussion in the Commons in 1860, was nearly lost by a disagreement between the two Houses, the numbers on a division in the House of Lords being seven and six. But we must not regard the House of Lords only in its legislative and judicial capacity. It has its sentimental side. The House of Lords, says Earl Russell, possesses an authority which can belong to no other body. "Nothing more excites reverence than ancient prescriptive privilege; nothing more moves the imagination than ancient lineage combined with recent achievement. Thus, to see in one assembly the descendants of the Talbots who fought in the fourteenth century and the Napier who so lately triumphed in Abyssinia; the heir of Marlborough who won the battle of Blenheim and of Wellington who was victor at Waterloo; of Nelson who fought at Trafalgar, of St Vincent and of Howe, of Cecil who advised Elizabeth, and of Grey who was minister of William IV., with the representatives of Mansfield, of Camden, of Hardwicke, and of Somers, gives dignity and weight to the House of Peers." The strength of the Upper House lies in what it is, in its combination of men deriving their titles and privileges from an illustrious and remote past with able men of the present day. But its power rests also on the wise behaviour of the peers themselves. They are not elected by counties or boroughs, nevertheless they represent the nation, as they have done with admirable effect from the days of Magna Carta downwards. Mixing in the world, they can feel the pulse of the people as a whole; and if the nation is carried away by a wild fit of religious or political passion, the House of Lords can appeal to the sober second-thought of the people, and can triumph through its ability to delay the national decision. Thus its origin, its historic associations, its constant infusion of new blood, its harmony with the spirit of the time, and its wise conduct in seasons of crisis, all combine to bestow on it an aggregate stability and strength that no mere hereditary chamber nor any elected senate could ever possess.

LECTURE IV.

THE COMMONS.

"As long as our sovereign lord the King, and his faithful subjects, the Lords and Commons of this realm—the triple cord which no man can break; the solemn, sworn constitutional frank pledge of this nation; the firm guarantee of each other's being and each other's rights; the joint and several securities, each in its place and order, for every kind and every quality of property and dignity—as long as these endure, so long we are all safe together, the high from the blights of envy and the spoliations of rapacity, the low from the iron hand of oppression and the insolent spurn of contempt."—BURKE.

"The House of Commons has combined national representation with the attributes of a senate. That peculiar union has, in our opinion, been owing to the variety of elements of which it is formed. Its variety of character has given to it its deliberative power, and it owes to its deliberative power its general authority."

"Notwithstanding the rapid changes amid which we live, and the numerous improvements and alterations we anticipate, this country is still Old England, and the past is one of the elements of our power."—DISRAELI.

GENTLEMEN,—This, my last lecture to you, is one which, from the very nature of its subject, cannot fail to be of interest to a body of Englishmen who wish to become acquainted with the history and constitution of the first representative assembly in the world—our House of Commons. Of the three Estates of the realm, it is the one which possesses most of the nation's sympathies, from the fact of its appealing directly to the people. The House of Commons is not limited to any privileged or exclusive order, but is essentially the House for the people —an assembly made for them, maintained by them, and in which they appear by right to legislate for the country. No wonder, then, that the House of Commons is the popular assembly, for the House of Commons nowadays means the nation. And fortunate, indeed, are we in possessing such an able exponent of our wishes and objections!

We think far from lightly of that same House of Commons. We look back upon its past history with pride and affection. We admit that to its courage and independence we owe much of the political liberty which we at present enjoy. Between our present freedom and the thraldom of the past stands the House of Commons, battling against tyranny, oppression, and political slavery,— often snubbed, sometimes cowed, but, with the stern endurance of Englishmen, seldom giving in till the success that waits upon pluck and perseverance was theirs, and the prize of England's freedom obtained. Ay, but it was a long and arduous struggle! The House of Commons was not always what it is now—the centre and force of the State. Step by step it gained those rights and privileges which it now possesses. Reign after reign it had to contend against monarchical tyranny and the oppression of servile courtiers, to maintain its position as an important branch of the legislature. For you must remember that before the Revolution of 1688 the Government of the country often signified only the Crown and a few royal parasites. The House of Commons was looked upon as a convenient sort of bank to grant supplies to the Crown, and be, in fact, the relieving officer of the Sovereign. When the King wanted money he summoned his Parliament; and if the Commons would not grant his request, there was a collision, then a dissolution, and the King levied taxes on his own account. The truth is, that before the institution of Parliamentary government, especially under the Stuarts, our monarchs tried to rule by their own absolute authority. You know how soon a custom becomes a right and a law. If I let you walk over my field (I haven't a field, but never mind) for twenty years, there is a right of way at once, and what was formerly a privilege becomes a right. So it was with our constitution. One King was permitted to do an unconstitutional act, and immediately it became a precedent to the next King; and the third King looked upon it as a right, and so in a very short time a host of excrescences appeared on the surface of the constitution—loans, benevolences, military despotism, unjust taxes, unjust judgments, unjust law-courts, and the like—which so concealed its original design that it became almost difficult to know what was law and what was not.

Trace back with me for a few moments the history of the rise and progress of our representative assembly, and see how gradual has been its system of development. In my last lecture I told you that the origin of Parliament was one of those things which " no fellow can understand," so I shall not trouble you with any antiquarian talk, but begin at once from the reign of Henry III., when the House of Commons made its first appearance as a legislative assembly. Its members were at first limited in their functions to " inquiring into grievances, and delivering their inquisition into Parliament," in which character they seem to have acted the part of commissioners rather than of popular representatives. They occupied the lower end of the chamber in which the barons and other magnates sat, but they did not mingle or vote in common with the peers. All they had to do was to consent to the taxes that had been imposed upon their constituents. I am afraid that the worthy burgesses and freeholders of those days did not at first fully appreciate the advantages of the representative system. In fact, so far from looking upon it as a privilege or a boon, we find that some boroughs considered it a downright nuisance, and that the electors neglected, and even refused, to send deputies to Parliament, on the ground of their own poverty and inability to defray the expenses of their representatives. For you must know that in those days, and down to a comparatively modern period, the members of the House of Commons received pay for their services. Notwithstanding, however, the modest position our first representatives held in Parliament, we find that as early as the next reign—that of Edward I.—they had behaved so well that a statute was passed enacting that "no tax should be levied without the joint consent of the Lords and Commons"—a statute of so much importance that to it is chiefly owing the great influence which the Lower House acquired in subsequent times. In the reign of Edward II. the Lords and Commons parted company, and the Commons, instead of hanging together humbly at the lower end of the council-hall, occupied a separate chamber. During the next reign, the result of having a big room all to themselves appears to have worked wonders with the Commons, for we find these three great constitutional principles laid down: 1. The illegality of raising money without the consent of Parliament; 2. The necessity for the concurrence of the Lords and Commons in any alteration of the law; and, 3. The right of the Commons to inquire into public abuses, and to impeach the Ministers of the Crown. In the reign of Richard II., though the Commons appear to have been too forgetful of their duties, and too submissively compliant with the wishes of the King, yet we find that they then acquired the important right of appropriating the public revenues to special purposes, and of inquiring into the mode of their expenditure. Constitutional principles acquired still further developments during the reign of Henry IV., for it was in this reign that the famous maxims were established, that "the Commons possess an exclusive right of originating all money bills," and that "the King ought not to take cognisance of any matter pending in Parliament."

The brief but memorable reign of Henry V., which shed an unfading lustre on English history, and to which we must ever look back with pride as one of the most brilliant periods in our annals, was not productive of any peculiar results in a constitutional point of view. The national mind was too much engrossed by military affairs, and by the contemplation of those glorious exploits which our arms had achieved on the Continent. It may, however, be mentioned, that owing to the great expenses incurred by Henry V. in the French wars, and the more readily to obtain supplies, he submitted his accounts to Parliament, " a circumstance which contributed in no slight degree to establish a regular correspondence between redress and supply, which for several centuries proved the balance-spring of the Constitution."

We now come to the period of the civil wars between the rival houses of York and Lancaster, when for many years the kingdom became a prey to intestine strife. And here the conduct of the Commons is not deserving of much respect. They betrayed a want of firmness and dignity ill-suited to the circumstances in which they were placed, veering and shifting according as either party became dominant, and in fact becoming "all things to all men." Owing to this vacillation they lost much of their moral weight and influence in the direction of public affairs; they acquired a lower tone and character, and became more subservient to the Crown, which found in them the ready and pliant instruments of its will. During the period of the Tudor dynasty, this servility of the Commons increased; and hence by degrees the constitution suffered from the inroads of arbitrary power, and the odious court of Star Chamber was erected, illegal taxes raised, and the nation tyrannised over in the most arbitrary manner. In fact, the fundamental principles of constitutional liberty were violated systematically and with impunity during the greater part of this period. Now and then the Commons objected, as when they opposed the claim of Henry VIII. to raise loans and benevolences, and boldly declared to Queen Elizabeth—who, by the way, called her faithful Commons "ignorant beasts"—that subsidies were a free gift and not a duty which she could exact; but still, on the whole, the Parliaments of those days were very servile assemblies, and vied with each other in exalting the royal dignity and in magnifying the

kingly office and prerogatives. The result of the
Reformation, too, had been to increase the power of
the Crown by making the King supreme head of
the Church as well as of the State. Henry VIII.,
therefore, and his immediate successors, held all but
unlimited sway over the destinies of their subjects,
and exacted from them a degree of submission
which had not been paid to any monarch since the
days of William the Conqueror. Nearly all the old
nobility who, in times of peril, would have presented
a barrier against the encroachments of arbitrary
power, had been swept away during the civil wars.
The entire constitution of the Upper House of Parliament had been changed, owing to the elimination of
the great majority of the dignified ecclesiastics and
heads of religious houses who had had seats therein
before the dissolution and the rupture with Rome.
Those who elected to remain behind, and who took
the oaths of supremacy, were for the most part
servile instruments in the hands of the sovereign—
who secured their services and their ready acquiescence by means of church and abbey lands.
Men thus bribed could have no independence, and
were powerless to defend the constitution and the
liberties of the nation. But before the death of
Queen Elizabeth a reaction had set in. The spirit

of liberty grew with the growing wealth and intelligence of the people—a spirit which the feeble struggles of James I. irritated instead of suppressed. And then came the Civil War. I am no admirer of Charles I., and up to a certain limit I admire the Parliament. I believe that Charles I. entertained a fixed purpose of destroying the old parliamentary constitution of England, and setting himself up as an absolute monarch — proceedings contrary, you know, to the fundamental principles of the Constitution. Then I don't admire the way he promised a thing and afterwards broke his promise,—as, for instance, in the Petition of Right; I dislike his pusillanimous conduct with regard to Strafford, the punishments inflicted by the Star Chamber, the ship-money, the death of Eliot, his attempt to sieze the five members, and the various other illegal measures he enforced, or endeavoured to enforce, during his reign; up to 1641 I approve of the conduct of the Parliament, and I look upon some of those members who at first opposed Charles I. as the true lovers of the constitution. But I do not approve of the demands of the Houses after 1641, and I think that in the war which ensued the Parliament were clearly the aggressors. We all know the result of that war. Charles Stuart was made the scapegoat, on whose head were laid, and in whose person were expiated, all the sins and misdeeds of his predecessors for more than a hundred years. With respect to the faction which persecuted him even to the death, but one opinion can now be formed. They were no friends to public liberty; for never, under the most arbitrary monarch, were the people of England subject to a more rigid tyranny; neither did they compose the majority of the nation, which, at least latterly, had recovered its reverence for the royal power. Even of the Commissioners appointed to sit in judgment on the King, scarcely one half could be induced to attend at his trial; and many of those who concurred in his condemnation subscribed the sentence with feelings of shame and remorse. But it is ever so in revolutions. A few violent men take the lead—their noise and their activity seem to multiply their numbers—and the great body of the people, either indolent or pusillanimous, are led in triumph at the chariot-wheels of a paltry faction.

We need not follow the Commonwealth beyond observing that the remnant of the Long Parliament, which scarcely numbered one hundred members, converted the kingdom for a brief period into a Republic, or what was tantamount to one. It abolished the House of Lords and the Established Church as well as the monarchy, and declared the supreme power vested in itself. It appointed a Council of State, consisting of forty-one members, which it invested with full executive power and authority to administer the affairs of the nation. This Executive Council was to hold office for the year, and was only responsible to Parliament for its acts. It must be said in favour of this Council that it set to work with considerable vigour to reform abuses and to amend the laws; and when we take into consideration the inexperience of its members in the conduct of public affairs, and their narrow-minded fanaticism, we are only surprised that their administration was marked by so much judgment and discretion. On the recall of Charles II. from exile the whole fabric of constitutional polity raised by Cromwell was however swept away, and the old constitution restored to its integrity. It was during the reign of Charles II. that indirect taxation was substituted for direct, the Feudal System finally extinguished, and the Habeas Corpus Act passed.

It is impossible to exaggerate the importance of this statute, which guarantees in the most distinct terms the immunity of the subject from illegal imprisonment. Taken in connection with trial by jury, it offers the most complete security that human laws can afford against the arbitrary infliction of punishment by the Sovereign. The reign of James II. is only memorable for his systematic attempts to overthrow the Constitution—attempts which finally resulted in the famous Revolution of 1688, which, by developing the system of Parliamentary government, transferred the centre and force of the State from the Crown to the House of Commons. The Revolution of 1688, however, only restored the British Constitution to its first principles. It did not enlarge the liberty of the subject, but simply gave it a better security. It neither widened nor contracted the foundation, but repaired and perhaps added a buttress or two to the fabric. Before 1688 the theory of our Constitution was, that the Crown was limited, and that its powers were checked by the Houses of Parliament; but this theory, as I have just shown, was not always recognised by the King in practice. The Revolution of 1688 brought the theory and practice into harmony, and since that time the Crown has never attempted to govern without Parliament. From 1688 to 1832 the control of the government of England was placed in the hands of the Great Governing Families, and the influence of the Peerage was immense. But the Reform Bills of 1832 and 1867 transferred much of this power to the middle classes, so that now the House of Commons, instead of being entirely filled by the nominees of powerful noblemen and by the representatives of the landed interest, is essentially the House of *Commons,* for in its ranks are commoners of all classes—country squires, professional men, manufacturers, merchants, and other followers of commerce. And here I trust parliamentary reform will stop. Thanks to the late Reform Bill, every one whose voice is in the slightest degree worth hearing can vote at an election, those only whose opinions are worthless being unrepresented, as I trust they will long remain. Parliamentary government is a machine of the most exquisite delicacy. A Government, such as ours, that yields and must yield to the slightest wish of the House of Commons, is only possible so long as that House of Commons is the organ of an "educated minority." Such an instrument of government has never yet been worked by a legislature chosen by the lowest classes.

The introduction of the King's Ministers into Parliament, which was accomplished in the reign of William III., gradually compelled the rival factions on both sides to have recourse to a system of party organisation. For parliamentary government is essentially government by party, since the condition of its existence is, that the Ministers of the Crown should be able to guide the decisions of Parliament, and especially of the House of Commons; and party organisation is the only means by which a popular assembly can be made to act steadily under recognised leaders. Now you know that in Parliament there are two great rival political parties—the one in favour of established *order*, and the other in favour of *change*. The order party we call *Conservatives*; the change party *Liberals*. Each of these parties is subdivided, the former into *Tories* and *Liberal Conservatives*; the latter into *Whigs* and *Radicals*. The Tories are men of uncompromising principles, and strongly attached to the *letter* of the Constitution. The Liberal Conservatives hold to the *spirit* rather than to the letter of the Constitution, which they seek to develop and perfect by advancing soberly and cautiously in the path of progressive improvement. The Whigs support the Constitution, but, at the same time, advocate its modification by new maxims of government, especially with regard to civil and religious liberty. The Radicals take their stand on the rights of man, and wish to remodel our constitution on the plan of American democracy.

They advocate universal suffrage, the separation of Church and State, the abolition of the House of Lords and all distinctions of rank, the exclusive taxation of property, and various other ideas, which they take every opportunity of promulgating.

Since 1688 these two schools of politics, with their subdivisions, have governed the nation. From 1688 to 1762 the Whigs were supreme in the State; the Tories from 1763 to 1830; and the Liberals from 1830 to the present time. Within the two last-mentioned periods of time, three great political questions have been decided—the first, Roman Catholic Emancipation; the second, Free Trade; and the third, Reform. Catholic disabilities came into existence in the reign of Charles II. Thereby all Papists were excluded from corporations, civil and military offices, and Parliament. After 1688 these disabilities were continued against the Popish supporters of the Stuarts with more or less severity till 1778, when the first relaxing statute in England was passed. On the union of England and Ireland, Pitt advocated Catholic Emancipation, and from 1800 to 1828 the measure was frequently contested; in fact, Emancipation Bills passed the Commons in 1812, 1813, 1821, and 1825, but on each occasion the Bill was rejected by the Lords. On the accession of Mr Peel in 1828, the Roman Catholics were finally relieved from all disabilities.

The principles of Free Trade were guaranteed by Magna Carta, but the towns were continually engaged in contests with foreign traders, which subsequently resulted in restricting foreign commerce, and protecting the home trade. In the reign of Henry VII. certain kinds of goods were forbidden to be imported except in English ships. In the reign of Elizabeth foreigners were shut out from the coasting trade. Under Cromwell the "Navigation Act" was passed, which prohibited the importation of merchandise from Asia, Africa, or America, except in English-built ships, and from Europe except in ships belonging to England or to the importing country. From 1688 to 1800 the system of heavy import duties became the fashion in England; prohibitory duties were imposed on foreign commodities, and the export of raw materials forbidden. In 1786, however, a treaty was concluded by Pitt with France, whereby all duties were reduced 50 per cent. After 1821 *moderate protection* was substituted for *prohibition*, and in 1821, 1824, and 1825 the Navigation Laws were relaxed; the wool duties were reduced in

1824; silk duties in 1826; and in 1828 the corn duties to free import at 70s. In 1842 the duties on 750 articles were reduced or abolished, and all raw materials liberated. In 1846 Sir Robert Peel became a convert to Free Trade, and the Corn-laws were happily abolished. The Navigation Laws were repealed in 1847, and from that time up to the present Free-trade principles have been applied to all articles of consumption.

Parliamentary Reform is a well-known cry. From Edward I. to Henry VIII. the House of Commons consisted of 74 knights and about 200 burgesses. Henry VIII. extended the right of election to Wales and to certain counties and towns in England, and increased the number of members by 33. From Edward VI. to James I., 147 members were added. Cromwell fixed the number of representatives at 400, giving the majority to the counties, contrary to the principle laid down by James I. From the Restoration to the reign of George III. the condition of our representative system was as rotten as it well could be. The corporations usurped the franchises of their boroughs, and were supported by the Crown and the House of Commons in their encroachments, so that a large number became what are called *close* boroughs, or boroughs in the hands of very limited and self-appointed bodies. Then there was another large class of boroughs called nomination boroughs, which were the absolute property of individuals, who disposed of the representation at pleasure. It was stated that 84 persons by their own authority sent 157 members to Parliament. The Duke of Norfolk was represented by 11 members; Lord Lonsdale by 9; Lord Darlington by 7; the Duke of Rutland, the Marquess of Buckingham, and Lord Carington, each by 6. The open boroughs chiefly depended on the votes of the Custom-house and Revenue officials, till the Marquess of Rockingham's Act of disfranchisement. Seats were openly bought and sold; towns with hardly any electors sent two members to Parliament; towns with large populations were unrepresented. Reform, indeed, was necessary. I cannot here enter into the various proposals for reform which were constantly suggested, and then as constantly rejected. I pass over the motions of Mr Pitt in 1782, 1783, and 1785; the motions of Mr Grey in 1793 and 1797; the disfranchisement of 84 Irish boroughs by the Union; the measures of Sir Francis Burdett from 1809 to 1819; the annual motions of the Whigs from 1820 to 1826; the enfranchisement of Leeds, Birmingham, and Manchester—and I come at once to the Reform Bill of 1832. You know what this bill did. It took away 143 seats from 56 disfranchised and 32 partially disfranchised boroughs. Of these seats, 64 were given to 42 new boroughs, and 65 to fresh divisions of the counties: the remainder were distributed between Scotland and Ireland, so that the English and Welsh counties were raised to 159 members against 337 borough members. Freeholders of the yearly value of £10, £10 householders, copyholders having an estate of £10 a-year, leaseholders of £50 with 20 years' leases, and tenants-at-will occupying lands or tenements paying a rent of not less than £50 a-year, were entitled to vote. But notwithstanding the improvements effected in our representative system by this measure, there still remained various defects. Many nomination boroughs still existed, the county members were still overbalanced by more than double their number of borough members, and the working classes were excluded. I must pass over the Chartist agitation from 1839 to 1848, the proposals of Mr Hume in 1848, of Mr Locke King in 1850, of Lord John Russell in 1852, 1854, and 1860, of Mr Disraeli in 1859, and of Mr Gladstone in 1866—for, after all, *the* Reform Bill of 1867 is the great measure that now interests us. And what has this bill done for us? It has extended the borough franchise to all occupiers of dwelling-houses who have resided for twelve months on the 31st July in any year, and have been rated to the poor-rates as ordinary occupiers; and to lodgers who have occupied, for the same period, lodgings of the annual value, unfurnished, of £10. Freeholders of the annual value of £5, instead of £10, are now entitled to vote. The franchise of copyholders and leaseholders has been reduced from £10 to £5, and the occupation franchise from £50 to £12. Forty-five seats were taken away—7 by disfranchisement of 4 bribing boroughs, and the rest by 1 seat each from 38 boroughs below a population of 10,000—and were distributed thus: 25 to English counties, 19 to English and Welsh boroughs, and 1 to the University of London. In the next session 7 more of the smallest English boroughs were disfranchised, and their seats transferred to Scotland. Reform Bills were passed in 1868 for Scotland and Ireland, and the total result of these Reform measures for the United Kingdom has been an increase of the electors from 1,350,000 to about 2,470,000, of whom about 750,000 belong to the working classes. The number of the members of the House of Commons now stands thus:—

For England and Wales, 493
Scotland, . . 60 (before 1832, 45;
after 1832, 53).
Ireland, . . . 105 (before 1832, 100).

Total, 658

Within the limits of this lecture it is impossible for me to discuss such matters as the passing of the Toleration Act, the repeal of the Test and Corporation Acts, the Abolition of Slavery, the Reform of our Criminal Law, the Disestablishment of the Irish Church, and various other measures which have been discussed, amended, or abolished by the House of Commons since its position as *the* great power in the State, owing to the development of parliamentary government. I must hasten on to the House of Commons itself, and tell you a little about it, who are its officers, what are its privileges, and how a debate is conducted within its walls, very much in the same way as I told you about the House of Lords. You are my audience, and I am to be the showman. Walk up, then, Gentlemen, and see the House of Parliament, which covers eight acres of ground on the shore of the Thames, which contains five hundred rooms, which cost only three millions of pounds sterling, and where laws are made for thirty millions of human beings. You obey my invitation, and (having already seen the House of Lords) we enter the House of Commons, thanks to a friendly member who has given us tickets for the Speaker's gallery. It is the night of a great debate, and the House is crowded in every part. In front of you is the Speaker, seated in his large green chair, in wig and gown. And a great man indeed is the Speaker of the House. He is chosen by the House of Commons from amongst its own members, subject to the approval of the Sovereign, and holds his office till the dissolution of the Parliament in which he was elected. His duties are, to read to the Sovereign petitions or addresses from the Commons, to deliver in the royal presence such speeches as are usually made on behalf of the Commons, to appoint tellers upon a division, to issue warrants for new writs to supply vacancies in Parliament, to inform the House upon the points of practice referred to him as they arise, and various other duties I need not trouble you' with. He reprimands those who have incurred the displeasure of the House, issues warrants of committal or release for breaches of privilege, expresses the thanks or approbation of the Commons to distinguished personages, and entertains the members of the House at dinner, in due succession, and at stated periods. As chairman of the House, he is the representative of order; and if a member perseveres in breaches of order, he may "name" him, as it is called,—a course uniformly followed by the censure of the House. But how the House shows its displeasure is a mystery. A gentleman, often out of order and often requiring the threat of being "named," asked the Speaker what would be the result of his naming him. "The Lord in heaven only knows!" replied the Speaker, which was an emphatic mode of confessing that nobody *did* know. For here you must remember that the members are only spoken of or spoken to by the title of the seat which they represent. The Speaker abstains from debating, unless in committee of the whole House; and he never votes on divisions except when the numbers happen to be equal, and then he gives the casting vote. The Speaker is subject to the authority of the House of Commons, and must not contravene it in deference to the Crown. Unless the House gives him leave, he cannot quit his chair. Thus, in 1621, the Speaker was admonished by several members for going out of the chair without the consent of the House, and was politely told that "he is but a servant to the House, not a master or a master's mate." It is his duty to utter the sense of the House; and should he refuse, it would be a breach of privilege. Thus, when Charles I. went to the House of Commons to arrest five of its members, and demanded of Mr Speaker Lenthall where they were, the Speaker replied, " I have neither eyes to see nor tongue to speak in this place but as the House is pleased to direct me, whose servant I am here; and I humbly beg your Majesty's pardon that I cannot give any other answer than this to what your Majesty is pleased to demand of me." When Parliament is prorogued, it is customary for the Speaker to address to the Sovereign in the House of Lords a speech recapitulating the proceedings of the session. The chief duty, however, of the Speaker is to keep order in the House; and indeed his office is no sinecure. He has to rule over a crowd of four hundred or five hundred gentlemen, often heated with party strife, often wandering from the point under discussion, and always wanting advice and guidance. No easy task that; and well he deserves, at the end of his official labours, to be rewarded with a peerage and a pension of £4000 for two lives.

On the right hand of the Speaker's chair is the Treasury bench, on which sit the members of the Administration. The front bench on the Speaker's left-hand side is reserved for the leading members of the Opposition, and behind them sit their followers. If you look carefully, you will see on the back of each seat a brass plate in which a member puts his card, thereby signifying that that seat belongs to him till the House rises. But no place can be secured in this manner unless the member has been present at prayers. Immediately after prayers each day, after Parliament has been opened, the Speaker counts the House, and if forty members are not present, he waits until four o'clock, when he again counts, and if the proper number has not arrived before he has ceased counting, he adjourns the House until the following sitting-day. If, during the debate, a member hints that forty members are not present, the debate is promptly stopped by the Speaker's cry of "Order! order!" the two-minute sand-glass is turned, the division bells are set ringing, and the doors of the House are thrown open. Then the Speaker counts the heads upon the benches, and if the required forty are not present, the House, debate and all, is closed for the evening. But the Speaker himself cannot notice that the House has fallen below the needful quorum—the hint must proceed from a member. Just below the Speaker, seated on three green chairs in front of the large solid oak table (that table which Mr Disraeli said he was so happy to see between him and Mr Gladstone), you see three gentlemen attired in wigs and gowns like barristers. These are the clerk and the assistant-clerks of the House of Commons. The Clerk of the House is one of the chief officers of the House of Commons. He has "to make true entries, remembrances, and journals of the things done and passed in the House of Commons;" he signs all orders of the House, endorses the bills, and reads whatever is required to be read in the House. He has the custody of all records and documents, and is responsible for the regulation of all matters connected with the business of the House in the several official departments under his control. Together with the clerk-assistants, he takes notes of the proceedings in the House in the minute-books on the table; and from these minutes the *votes* which are ordered to be printed are made up, under the direction of the Speaker. At the end of the session the *Journal* is properly made out from the minute-books, the printed votes, and the original papers that have been laid before the House. On the left-hand side of the clerk of the House sit the clerk-assistants.

At the other end of the table, exactly opposite the clerks, is the silver-gilt mace, which is always placed on the table during the sitting of the House, with the Speaker in the chair. When the Speaker is accompanied by what Cromwell called "that bauble," he has the power to order persons into custody for disrespect or other breaches of privilege committed in his presence, without any previous order of the House. On the Speaker's entrance to or departure from the House, the mace is borne before him by the Serjeant-at-Arms; and when the mace is not in the House, it remains with the Speaker, and accompanies him upon all state occasions. When the Speaker leaves the chair, on the House going into Committee, the mace is removed from the table and placed under it. What debates that mace has listened to, what witnesses it has heard examined, and what numbers it has seen ordered into custody, whilst lying innocently on the shoulders of the serjeant-at-arms! It is a very old member, too, of the House—in fact, the oldest member, for it is over 200 years old. Do you see that gentleman seated in an immense chair, like two dentists' chairs rolled into one, just beneath the Speaker's gallery, and close to the bar of the House? Well, that is an awful official of the House of Commons—no less a man than the Serjeant-at-Arms. He has to attend the Speaker with the mace on entering and leaving the House, or going to the House of Lords, or attending her Majesty with addresses. He has to keep clear the gangway at the bar and below it; to take strangers into custody who are irregularly admitted into the House, or who misconduct themselves; to introduce with the mace peers or judges attending within the bar, and messengers from the Lords; to bring to the bar prisoners to be reprimanded by the Speaker, or persons in custody to be examined as witnesses, and various other duties I need not particularise. Out of the House of Commons he has to execute all warrants for the commitment of persons ordered into custody by the Commons. In the execution of all these duties he is assisted by a Deputy-Serjeant.

And now let me introduce you to the members of the Fourth Estate—the reporters for the newspapers. What should we do without those hard-working Parliamentary historians? What would the voice of Parliament be if its debates were not scattered over the land by means of the newspapers? There they sit night after night, those busy reporters, writing down words at the rate of 100 a minute for their respective papers, in their little cells in the gallery above the Speaker's chair. No matter at what time the debate closes, the next morning at our breakfast-table there is our 'Times' or our Penny Paper full of last night's speeches, and perhaps a leading article on the debate itself. To think that every word those hard-working reporters write is a "breach of privilege"! Yet so it is, for as I told you in my last lecture on the Lords, the publication of debates in Parliament is prohibited, though, of course, this prohibition is merely nominal, and the sooner it is annulled the better. Just above the reporters' gallery is the ladies' gallery, screened by an iron grating, whence fair ladies look down upon their lords below, and yet cannot be seen by them.

Now, as I think I have pointed out to you the chief objects of attraction that at first strike your eye in the House of Commons, let me give you an insight into how a debate is conducted. Every matter is determined upon "questions" put to the Speaker, and resolved in the affirmative or negative as the case may be. When a member proposes a question it is called "moving the House," or, more commonly, "making a motion;" and in order to give the House due notice of his intention, the form of the motion is stated on a previous day, and entered in the order-book or notice paper. Monday, Thursday, and Friday are set apart for the Government orders, Wednesday for the orders of independent members, and Tuesday for notices of motions. After a motion has been submitted to the House, it must be seconded by another member, otherwise it is immediately dropped. When the motion has been seconded, it merges in the question, which is then proposed by the Speaker to the House, and read by him. The House is now said to be "in possession of the question," and must dispose of it one way or another before it can proceed with any other business. If the House wishes to evade or supersede the question, it has the choice of four good "dodges." First, a member may get up in the midst of the debate and move "that this House do *now* adjourn;" and if this motion be resolved in the affirmative, the House immediately adjourns, and all business for that day is at an end. The second plan is to move (if it is a day on which notices of motions have precedence) "that the orders of the day be now read;" and if this be carried in the affirmative, the House immediately proceeds with the orders of the day, and the original question is superseded. The "previous question," as it is called, is the third ingenious method of avoiding a vote upon any question that has been proposed.

At the close of a debate, or when there is no debate, the Speaker "puts the question," without any direction from the House, but by a motion for the previous question this act of the Speaker may be intercepted. The words of this motion are, "that that question"—*i.e.*, the proposed question—"be *now* put." If the previous question be negatived, the House thereby decides that the principal question to which it relates shall not be put from the chair at that time. If, however, it be carried, the principal question is accordingly put from the chair without further debate. Sir Harry Vane is said to be the first contriver of the previous question, hence an M.P. in the reign of Charles II. said in debate that "this previous question is like the image of the inventor—a perpetual disturbance." In a committee of the House there can be no previous question, but if it be wished to avoid the question, it is usual to move that "the chairman do leave the chair." The fourth mode of intentionally avoiding a question is by moving the omission of all the words of the question after the word "that" at the beginning, and by the substitution of other words of a different import, and thus making a new question. When, however, all preliminary objections are disposed of, the question must next be "put." The Speaker rises from his chair and states or reads to the House a copy of the question, beginning with, "The question is that;" and this form is always observed, and precedes every vote of the House. When the question has been "put," the Speaker takes the sense of the House by desiring that "as many as are of that opinion say *ay*, and as many as are of the contrary opinion say *no*." This done, the Speaker endeavours to judge which party has the majority from the loudness of the opposing exclamations, and expresses his opinion by saying, "I think the *ayes* have it;" or, "I think the *noes* have it." If all acquiesce in his decision, the question is said to be "resolved in the affirmative" or "negative," as the case may be; but if his decision is disputed, a division ensues. And here let me say a few words about this division, or, in other words, how the vote of the House of Commons is taken. The chamber for debate is, as you know, a large square room, and on each side is flanked by two long corridors called the division lobbies. When the Speaker has commanded the House to divide, every member leaves his seat, and, if he is an *ay*, passes up the House and circles round the Speaker's chair into the western lobby; but if he is a *no*, he takes the contrary direction, and files round into the eastern lobby. When all are penned into the division-lobbies, the names of the voters are taken down, and the number counted, and then the members return again to the House. The four tellers who have counted the numbers push towards the Speaker's chair, and the Speaker formally announces the decision of the House. And we who have waited in the lobby outside on great-debate nights, when a division has ensued, know the shouts after shouts with which the winners echo back their delight.

When a member speaks in the Commons he addresses the Speaker, and he must not direct his speech to the House, or to any party on either side of it. He must stick to the question under discussion, and if he wanders from the point he is sure to be interrupted by cries of "Question," and the Speaker will desire him "to speak to the question." Once having addressed the House, he cannot speak twice on the same subject, except to explain where he has been misunderstood; but in a Committee of the House he may speak as often as he pleases, and that with some members is painfully often. During the debate he is not to read books or newspapers, and not to interrupt members when speaking by hissing, or other unseemly noises. He is not to walk about the House or stand at the bar during the debate, and when he enters or leaves the House he must take off his hat out of respect to the chair. Some of these rules are not always strictly obeyed; and we all know when that illustrious Protestant whom Peterborough delighteth to honour as its representative gets upon his legs to speak, his appearance is the signal for a regular "row," which is decidedly unparliamentary.*

But it is not only in debate that a member can show how deserving he is of the selection of his constituents. The work of the House of Commons is carried on chiefly in committees, and a member who is useful in committees is quite as efficient a member of the House as a debater. Of these committees there are several. First, there is a "Committee of the whole House," which is, in fact, the House itself, presided over by a chairman instead of by the Speaker. It may be appointed to consider certain resolutions as to the nature of which considerable latitude prevails; or the House re-

* During the session of 1870 Mr Bentinck brought a complaint against Mr Otway for quoting, in a recent debate on the Tornado, a document which he had subsequently refused to lay on the table; and Mr Disraeli laid down the Parliamentary rule, in which Mr Gladstone concurred, *that when a Minister quotes from a paper it becomes public property ipso facto.*

solves itself into such committee to consider the details of a bill, the principle of which may be discussed at any or all of its other stages. "The Committee of Ways and Means," which inquires into the funds by which the expenditure of the nation is to be sustained, is always one of the whole House: so is the "Committee of Supply." I must say a few words about this Committee of Supply. All bills relating to public income or expenditure originate with the Commons, and all bills authorising expenditure of the public money are based upon resolutions moved in a Committee of Supply, granting to the Crown the sums requisite for defraying the expenses attendant on the various branches of the public service. These resolutions are reported to the House, and adopted or rejected; and, at the end of the Session, are consolidated in the Appropriation Bill. Secondly, there is a "Select Committee," chosen by ballot or otherwise, for some specific purpose: its numbers seldom exceed twenty or thirty members, and occasionally it is declared a committee of secrecy. And, thirdly, there are "Committees on Private Bills." So that it by no means follows, because a member's name does not appear as taking an active part in the debates of the House, that he is a faithless representative of his constituents.

He may never once have spoken in Parliament, and yet be as useful a member as the House possesses, from constantly being engaged on committees. A friend of mine, one of the oldest members of the House of Commons, during the whole time of his membership never once spoke in the House, and yet his presence was eagerly desired in the committee-rooms. But if you find a man who never speaks in debate, and whose name never appears on committees, you may certainly put him down as a "muff"—as one of the rank and file, who is a mere voting machine, and blind follower of the wishes of his leaders.

It is not every man who can speak in Parliament, even though he be far from deficient in ability. The House of Commons is a very formidable audience to face, till habit has removed fear. Those gentlemen whom you see lolling about the benches with their hats on, and looking on ordinary occasions as if they were awfully bored, are the coldest, hardest, and most practical of listeners; and many a new member who has risen in his place to give the House the benefit of his opinions on the question under discussion, has failed most signally from sheer nervousness. A member rose up one night to speak, but all he could say was, "Sir, I conceive—I conceive—I say, sir, I conceive," and then stopped short as if aghast at his eloquence. A member at once rose, and, amid the laughter of the whole House, said, "Sir, the honourable gentleman has conceived three times, and *brought forth nothing.*" Another member began his speech thus: "Mr Speaker, sir, I observe to wish—I mean, sir, I wish to observe, that—that, sir" (a long pause), "I will sit down." Sometimes a member gets up who feels by no means influenced by constitutional modesty: thus one man began to speak by addressing the House as "Gentlemen," which is very unparliamentary, because, as I have just said, the Speaker is always to be addressed, and not the House. He was immediately called to account, and "Order, order!" rang through the chamber. Nothing disconcerted, the member simply said, "Oh, you don't consider yourselves gentlemen then; I beg your pardon, I'm sure," and then went on with his speech according to the rules of the House. But because a member fails in his maiden speech, it does not follow that his parliamentary career will be a failure. Some thirty years ago, a young member, who had made a name in the world as a wit and novelist, rose up in the House. His speech provoked the laughter of all, and he sat down amid derisive cheers. That young member is now our distinguished Conservative leader, Mr Disraeli.

I need hardly tell you that every Act of Parliament begins as a *bill* in Parliament. A bill in Parliament is simply a law in preparation. Now bills are either *public*, such as when they affect the general interests of the State; or *private*, such as bills to enable private individuals to associate together to undertake works of public utility at their own risk, and, in a degree, for their own benefit, or for perfecting titles to estates, &c. Public bills, unless money bills, and those affecting the Peerage, may originate in either House. A bill must pass through three stages—the first, second, and third readings. Before the invention of printing, each bill was actually read aloud three times over in both Houses of Parliament, and hence that expression, a "reading." After each reading the Speaker states when the next stage will be taken. The introduction of the bill may be opposed at once, as the bill itself may at any stage. After the second reading, the bill is considered in committee of the whole House; and it is there debated clause by clause, amendments may be made, and sometimes it is entirely remodelled. Should the bill be wholly objectionable, its opposers propose that it be read a second time upon "this day six months," which is a delicate way of kicking it out altogether. A bill rejected in this manner cannot be reintroduced in the same session. But let us suppose that it has not been rejected, and has gone satisfactorily through committee. The chairman of the committee then reports it to the House, with such amendments as the committee have made, and the House reconsiders the whole bill, and the question is put upon every amendment. The bill, having passed and been reprinted, and the title settled, is decorously tied up and carried to the House of Lords where it passes precisely through the same forms as in the Commons. Should a difference arise with regard to the bill between the Lords and the Commons, a conference usually follows between members deputed from either House, who, for the most part, settle and adjust the disagreement. But if both Houses remain inflexible, the bill is dropped for the session.

When the bill has passed through both Houses in this manner, it is deposited in the House of Lords (except in the case of a Bill of Supply) to await the Royal Assent, which is given either by her Majesty in person or by commission. When her Majesty gives her consent in person, her concurrence is pre viously communicated to the clerk-assistant, who reads the titles of the bills, on which the royal assent is signified by a gentle inclination. If it be a bill of supply, the clerk pronounces loudly, "*La reigne remercie ses bons sujets, accepte leur bénévolence, et ansi le veult*"—" The Queen thanks her good subjects, accepts their benevolence, and answers, 'Be it so.'" To other public bills the form of assent is "*La reigne le veult*"—" The Queen wills it so." To private bills, "*Soi fait comme il est désiré,*—" Be it as it is prayed." When the royal assent is refused, the clerk says, "*La reigne s'avisera,*"—" The Queen will consider of it;" but these words are never now pronounced, and have not been heard since Queen Anne refused to sanction the Scotch Militia Bill in the year 1707.

So far, Gentlemen, I have endeavoured briefly to show you what are the proceedings and usages in the House of Commons. Of course there are a hundred things I have not said which I might have said, but within the brief limits of a lecture I think I have told you enough to give you some idea of what goes on in that important house down at Westminster. And now let us see who are qualified to be our representatives, so that we may not give our votes to the wrong persons, and thus make ourselves ridiculous, and those whom we may select. To obtain a seat in the House of Commons is the ambition of most Englishmen. For this end, many men give up their professions or their business, and spend small fortunes in the attempt. Those of you who know anything about elections know how eagerly the contest is carried on between the rival candidates for a county or a borough; what excitement, what speeches, what "blarney," what "fights" and rows and personalities there are on those occasions! And for what? Simply and solely for the honour of being in Parliament. Besides the honour of the thing, and the satisfaction of a just ambition and of a wish to enjoy the sense of power, little else is to be gained. A member of Parliament receives no pay for his services,—not even when he sits on committees, as many people imagine. His time is spent in real hard dry labour, either in the House or in committee-rooms. The days are past when he might have had his share of snug sinecures, pensions, and other pickings out of the nation's pocket. Even such Government posts as are open to him are neither many nor lucrative; and as for the great prizes in the Ministry, they are held only while the Government whose views he supports are in office. In a pecuniary point of view, then, a man entering Parliament has little to gain; but apart from this he has much to gain. Other men by their newspaper articles, their books, or their out-of-door speeches, may influence indirectly the country, but a member of Parliament influences it directly. By his vote, national education may be given to thousands, open vice may be repressed, wrongs may be redressed, sickness and disease be warded off, religion be more freely disseminated; and, in fact, there is no end to the good it is in his power to effect. No wonder, then, that a seat in Parliament should be an object of ambition to so many. But this ambition is not open to all: not every one is entitled to put his finger in the legislative pie, and to write his influence upon the face of the country. A man who is an alien—that is, one born out of the kingdoms of England, Scotland, or Ireland, or the dominions belonging to those kingdoms —cannot be a member of Parliament. If a man is under twenty-one years of age he cannot be elected. Neither can a man who is of unsound mind, nor English nor Scotch peers; though Irish peers, unless elected as one of the representative peers of Ireland, may sit for any place in Great Britain. Again, the English, Scotch, and Irish judges (the Master of the Rolls excepted) are disqualified, together with those holding places of profit under the Crown. Clergymen, whether belonging to the English, Scottish, or

Roman Catholic Churches, are incapable of being elected. Any one who indirectly or directly undertakes any contract with a Government department (except contractors for Government loans) is disqualified from sitting in Parliament. A person attainted of treason or felony, being dead in law, is also disqualified. When a member becomes a bankrupt he is incapable of sitting and voting (unless the creditors be paid) for twelve months, and at the end of that time his election is void. Such are the chief grounds of disqualification for sitting in the House of Commons. By the law of Parliament, a member already returned for one place is ineligible for any other until his first seat is vacated; and hence it is the practice for a member desiring to represent some other place to accept the Chiltern Hundreds, or other similar office under the Crown, in order to render himself eligible at the election. Again, it is a settled principle of parliamentary law, that a member after he is duly chosen cannot relinquish his seat; and so, in order to evade this restriction, a member who wishes to retire accepts office under the Crown, a proceeding which legally vacates his seat, and obliges the House to order a new writ. The offices usually selected are those of Steward of her Majesty's three Chiltern Hundreds, or of the manors of East Hendred, Northstead, or Hempholme, or of Escheator of Munster; and they are resigned again as soon as their purpose is effected.

As the House of Lords has its privileges, so has the House of Commons. The House of Commons, as a constituent part of the High Court of Parliament, has the power to commit for contempt, and the courts of law cannot inquire into the grounds of judgment, but must leave the person committed to suffer the punishment which the House awards. Thus in 1751 a Mr Murray was committed to Newgate by the Commons for contempt, and was brought before the Court of King's Bench by a *habeas corpus*. The court refused to admit him to bail; and in subsequent cases the law decided that when the House of Commons adjudges anything to be a contempt or a breach of privilege, "its adjudication is a conviction, and its commitment an execution, and that courts of justice have no cognisance of the acts of the Houses of Parliament." However, the dicta of judges respecting privilege of Parliament have been very conflicting. In the majority of cases the judges have refused to adjudicate in any manner on questions of privilege, and during the last century the current authorities were strongly opposed to any such adjudication. But later decisions have been much more favourable to the power of Courts of Law in this respect. The House of Commons cannot merely by a resolution of its own create privileges. The chief breaches of privilege are, refusal to release persons entitled to the privilege of the House when detained in custody; open resistance to the officers of the House in the execution of their duty; absconding when summoned by the House; discharging persons committed by the House; impleading in courts of law persons entitled to privilege; prosecuting for words or actions spoken or done under the authority of the House; and writing or saying anything derogatory to the honour of the House, or any of its members. The present mode of punishment adopted by the Commons for contempt or breach of privilege is to commit the offender to the custody of the Serjeant-at-Arms to Newgate during the pleasure of the House, and to keep him there till he presents a petition praying for his release, and expressing contrition for his offence. He is then brought to the bar, and, usually after a reprimand from the Speaker, is discharged on payment of certain fees. It was formerly the practice to make prisoners receive the judgment of the House kneeling at the bar, but this has long since been discontinued. Prisoners committed by the Commons are immediately released from confinement on a prorogation of Parliament.

All members of the House of Commons have perfect freedom of speech in Parliament; and though this privilege was frequently violated by the power of the Crown in former times, yet it seems to have been recognised as part of the law of the land from a very early date. For we read that in the reign of Edward III. the Commons debated among themselves concerning the King's prerogative, and yet were never interrupted in their consultations. In the reign of Richard II. a member of the Commons was condemned as a traitor for words spoken in Parliament; but on the accession of Henry IV. the judgment was reversed, as being "against the law and custom which had been before in Parliament." And again, in 1512, another member was prosecuted for having introduced certain bills, and accordingly fined and imprisoned; but the judgment was also reversed, and an Act passed protecting members from being questioned in other courts for their proceedings in Parliament. The last occasion on which the privilege of freedom of speech was directly impeached was in the celebrated case of Sir John Eliot and others; and the prosecution of these members was one of the illegal acts which hastened the fate of Charles I. Freedom of speech was finally confirmed in 1688 by the Bill of Rights, which declared "that the freedom of speech and debates or proceedings in Parliament ought not to be impeached or questioned in any court or place out of Parliament." But though a member may not be questioned out of Parliament, he is liable to censure and punishment by the House of which he is a member. And there have been numerous instances of members having been admonished, imprisoned, and some even expelled from the House of Commons, for offensive words spoken before the House. In modern times, members who offend against propriety are called to order, and generally satisfy the House with an explanation or apology.

A third great privilege which the Commons enjoy is freedom from arrest and molestation. This privilege is of great antiquity. At the end of the sixth century we read that it was one of the laws of Ethelbert that "if the King call his people to him (in the Witena-gemot), and any one does an injury to one of them, let him pay a fine." In the reign of Edward I. that King said, "It does not seem fit that the King should grant that they who are of his council should be distrained in time of Parliament." It would be beyond my purpose to tell you all the statutes that have been passed in various reigns confirming this privilege; suffice it to say that the freedom of members from arrest has become rather a legal right than a parliamentary privilege. Formerly this privilege extended to the servants of members, but this is now abolished. It must, however, be clearly understood that this freedom from arrest is limited only to civil and not to criminal causes. For any indictable offence—such as treason, felony, or breach of the peace—privilege of Parliament cannot be claimed. Witnesses, petitioners, and others, whilst in attendance upon Parliament, are also protected by privilege from molestation, threats, or legal proceedings. A member of Parliament, owing to his privilege not rendering him liable to attachment, cannot be admitted as bail, because, in the event of the recognisances being forfeited, he could not be effectually proceeded against. And as a member's attendance in Parliament is so important, it is held to supersede the obligation of attendance in other courts —that is to say, he need not serve on juries, and in former times he was exempt from being served with a subpœna, but that privilege is not now enforced. One important privilege which formerly belonged to the Commons has been lately abolished—that of trying all petitions against elections. This is now dealt with by three Election Judges chosen annually in rotation from the Courts of Queen's Bench, Common Pleas, and Exchequer. But, as we have just seen in the case of Donovan O'Rossa, because the House of Commons has handed over a certain authority to the Judges, it is not deprived of all power respecting the election of its members.

And now, Gentlemen, I must draw this lecture to a conclusion; but before leaving you, let me briefly allude to the power of Parliament. I have already said that no bill can become an Act of Parliament till it has received the royal assent; that no bill can be presented for the royal signature till it has received the sanction of both Houses of Parliament; and that thus, before any measure can become a law in this country, it must receive the consent of three distinct voices. But, say you, are there no limits to these three governing powers—Queen, Lords, and Commons—which conjointly constitute Parliament, when they act in unison? Gentlemen, the authority of Parliament is almost boundless. A statesman once said, Parliament can do anything *but make it rain.* Sir Edward Coke says, its power is "so transcendent and absolute, that it cannot be confined, either for causes or persons, within any bounds." The authority of Parliament extends over the United Kingdom and all its colonies and foreign possessions. It has no other limits to its power of making laws for the whole Empire than those which are common to it and to all other sovereign authority—the willingness of the people to obey or their power to resist them. It has the power to alter the Constitution of the country, for that is the Constitution which the last Act of Parliament has made. It may take away life by acts of attainder, and make an alien as a natural-born subject. It has changed the professed religion of the country, and has altered the hereditary succession to the throne. And, indeed, there is little it can *not* do.

Parliament does not, however, in the ordinary course, legislate directly for the colonies. For some the Queen in Council legislates, and others have legislatures of their own, and propound laws for their internal government, subject to the approval of the Queen in Council; but these may be afterwards repealed or amended by statutes of the Imperial Parliament. Such, in a few words, is what Parliament can do. And, Gentlemen, when you consider that this boundless power may be exercised either for the wellbeing or detriment of the State, and how sacred a responsibility is intrusted to the hands of a fallible community, I am sure you will all agree with me that the more our legislators are illumined by the light of God's wisdom, the better for them and for us.

I conclude these Lectures which I have had the pleasure of delivering to you by a quotation from a memorable speech of the late Mr Canning, which, to my mind, ought to be taken as the model of Conservative statesmanship. He says, "I consider it to be the duty of a British statesman, in internal as well as external affairs, to hold a middle course between extremes; avoiding alike extravagances of despotism or the licentiousness of unbridled freedom; reconciling power with liberty; not adopting hasty or ill-advised experiments, or pursuing any airy or unsubstantial theories; but not neglecting, nevertheless, the application of sound and wholesome knowledge, and pressing with sobriety and caution into the service of his country any generous and liberal principles, whose excess indeed may be dangerous, but whose foundation is in truth. This, sir, in my mind, is the true conduct of a British statesman; but they who resist indiscriminately all improvement as innovation may find themselves compelled at last to submit to innovations although they are not improvements."

THE END.

www.ingramcontent.com/pod-product-compliance
Lightning Source LLC
Chambersburg PA
CBHW020811230426
43666CB00007B/964